THE INSTITUTE OF
CHARTERED FINANCIAL ANALYSTS:

A TWENTY-FIVE YEAR HISTORY

THE INSTITUTE OF CHARTERED FINANCIAL ANALYSTS:

A TWENTY-FIVE YEAR HISTORY

Nancy Regan

 The Institute of Chartered Financial Analysts

ISBN 0-935015-00-0 (casebound)
ISBN 0-935015-01-9 (paperbound)

Printed in the United States of America

TABLE OF CONTENTS

PREFACE

It is interesting to note that the time from Ben Graham's first proposal for certification until the Institute awarded its first charters is roughly equal to the time from the award of those first charters until today. Most of us are familiar with the recent history of the Institute, but the pre-Institute history, the organization and the early years, the struggle to formulate the body of knowledge, the exam program and the first efforts at continuing education, can easily be forgotten. It is a tribute to the Institute's current leaders that they commissioned this book to preserve that history and to serve as a guide to all those who will come after.

The vast amount of material to be reviewed and the pressure of available time suggested that an independent researcher and author was needed. Pete Morley found the ideal person. Nancy Regan dug into the archives with enthusiasm, aided by the reminiscences of past executive directors, presidents and others. To the task she brought both a research talent and a felicity of writing. She not only has produced a well-researched history, but she has told the story in a thoroughly readable fashion, demonstrating clearly her own interest in the subject.

In May 1984, when Jay Vawter asked me to oversee the preparation of this history, I found the challenge irresistible. Abe Kulp, who more than anyone else made professional certification a reality and got the ICFA started, was my boss at Wellington from 1950 to 1966. During those years, I was well aware of his efforts to establish certification and often discussed the difficulties and problems with him. Then, after receiving my own charter in 1965, I became a member of the ICFA Research and Publications Committee. Since then, in one capacity or another, I have been actively associated with some Institute activity. It has been a great personal pleasure to review again the story of those years and to have a small part in preparing the history of the Institute to date. My only regret is the inability to acknowledge the individual contributions of everyone—initiators, trustees, committee members, graders, and staff—who made the program and the Institute what they are today.

In particular, it was good once again to recall the major contributions of Abe Kulp not just in getting the Institute started, but also in helping set the high standards that have characterized its existence. It is altogether appropriate that this history be dedicated to him. It also is worth remembering the work of that distinguished scholar and true gentleman, Nick Molodovsky, who worked so hard to contribute to the profession and help define the initial body of knowledge. It was my great privilege to have known and worked with both of them; together they contributed mightily to the early years of the profession, long before it achieved the academic interest it has today, long before it had a body of knowledge, and long before it was recognized as a profession at all. "Giants were on earth in those days," and they serve as a model for us for the future.

We can only speculate on the future of the Institute. What changes in society, in government, in financial organizations, and in capital markets will take place, and what will be the contribution of the financial analyst? Imagine what the history of the second 25 years will be like! Financial analysts undoubtedly will make a contribution—and many of those who recently received their charters will be among the leaders. I hope that this volume will provide both background and inspiration for their efforts.

Edmund A. Mennis, CFA
Palos Verdes, California
July 14, 1986

INTRODUCTION

When I became chairman of the Board of Trustees of the Institute of Chartered Financial Analysts in April 1984, much as those assuming such responsibilities are wont to do, I found myself reflecting upon my own long-standing personal involvement with the Institute and what it had meant to my professional career. Like most, my involvement with the Institute began as a candidate, back in the mid 60s, shortly after the founding of the Institute.

These reflections led me to realize that the Institute was no longer an infant, a child, or even a teenager, but clearly had matured to adulthood. Furthermore, a little investigation turned up the fact that the Institute was rapidly approaching its Silver Anniversary. This finding proved a bit perplexing, as there are several possible dates one might consider in identifying the Institute's beginnings. First, on June 14, 1959, the Financial Analysts Federation Board of Directors approved its establishment. However, the actual organizing of the Institute took somewhat longer than perhaps had been initially envisioned, and it was the fall of 1961 before things really began to happen. On January 30, 1962, the Institute was incorporated and went "live." Another date of interest is June 15, 1963, when the first examinations were given.

In terms of determining this important 25th Anniversary, my own preference is for January 30, 1962, because on that day the Institute was no longer a dream, a concept or a vague hope, but truly became a reality that was, over time, to have a major impact on the investment profession.

My musings in the spring of 1984 then led to the idea that this anniversary was truly a significant event for the Institute and a good opportunity to record for historical purposes its founding, early development, and major growth as a dynamic factor in the investment profession.

When I proposed this idea to the Board, it was greeted enthusiastically; and now, as the Institute celebrates its Silver Anniversary, you hold this history in your hand.

I did not have to think long about who should be the editor of the book—Ed Mennis, who has truly been a giant in the Institute's history. He was one of its early presidents and served a long and distinguished career as editor of *The CFA Digest*. When I asked Ed to undertake this task, he accepted readily and with great enthusiasm. In the preface of this book he gives you some of his own thoughts in that regard.

The timing of this publication was fortunate. Many of those persons who had been so much involved in the Institute's founding were still around, but beginning to pay the high price of advancing years. Abe Kulp, perhaps the most vital force behind the founding of the Institute, passed away shortly after this history was begun, but his son, Charles Kulp, himself a CFA of long standing, graciously provided to the Institute all of his father's papers and correspondence relating to the ICFA. Had we begun this project even six months later, it is likely his father's papers would have been destroyed. Our author, Nancy Regan, will tell you that without those papers this history would have been seriously diluted.

You will shortly discover, as you read this book, that the Institute's growth as an educational organization and a major, dynamic force in our profession today, was hardly anticipated by its founding fathers. In fact, they hoped the Institute might grant as many as 200 charters in the first 10 years of its life. That number was exceeded in the first year, and as we enter the 25th year there are more than 9,000 charters outstanding and over 6,000 candidates enrolled in the examination program!

As the number of charters began to overwhelm even the most optimistic forecast, it became increasingly clear that the educational function of the Institute could no longer focus entirely on its candidates, but must broaden out to its members, as well. This has led in recent years to a greatly expanded continuing education program and the establishment in 1985 of a voluntary accreditation program.

Although the Institute has always been international in character, encompassing both the United States and Canada from its very inception, it gradually took on a truly international flavor with candidates applying from various points around the world. As the 1980s came along, this trend accelerated, reflecting the dramatic economic and financial shrinkage of the world. In the fall of 1984 the Institute formally recognized this by establishing an International Committee so that we might be better prepared to fulfill our responsibilities, not just as a North American organization, but as a truly global institution. As this book goes to publication, the Institute within the past two years has had a number of meetings with investment analyst organizations around the world. It has sponsored a seminar jointly with the London Society of Investment Analysts, has become involved with the International Coordinating Committee, is looking forward to participating in October 1986 in the bi-annual conference of the European Federation of Financial Analysts Societies, and is planning a seminar to be held in Singapore. All of this gives one great pause to contemplate what the next 25 years may hold.

If you are one of the older hands around the Institute, as I am, and have been involved with it in one way or another for a significant portion of its life, please read this with reminiscence, a sense of history, perhaps a bit of nostalgia, and more importantly, thoughtful reflection on what this fine organization may have contributed to your own professional growth.

If, on the other hand, you are a relatively new member of the Institute, perhaps after reading this history you will have a better appreciation for the immense volunteer effort that has gone on before you that has made it possible for you to enjoy the many benefits that accrue to all members of the Institute of Chartered Financial Analysts.

Jay Vawter
Princeton, N.J.
June 10, 1986

For A. Moyer Kulp, CFA,
whose patience and persistence
made the Institute a reality.

ACKNOWLEDGEMENTS

The voluntary efforts of those who made the Institute successful have guided and facilitated my work throughout this project. It is with pleasure that I acknowledge their help.

For information about the Institute's prehistory and early days, I thank Mildred Herman of the Financial Analysts Federation for sorting through that organization's files, and Charles Kulp for the generous donation of his father Abe Kulp's papers. I am also grateful to many of those involved in the Institute's beginnings, including Lucien O. Hooper, Ragnar Naess, William Norby, Ray Smith, George Hansen and David Watterson.

For written and oral reminiscences, I am indebted to the Institute's three Executive Directors—Scott Bauman, Whit Broome, and most of all, Stewart Sheppard—who were exceedingly supportive of the project. The papers of the Institute's officers and committee chairmen also provided me with a unique perspective on the ICFA. David Williams, Mary Petrie, Walter Stern, Philip Brooks, James Vertin, Jay Vawter, Hap Butler, Carl Beckers, Harvey Earp, Richard Lambourne, and Gilbert Palmer all made significant contributions.

To the ICFA staff, I owe a substantial debt of gratitude for research assistance and moral support. I thank Peggy Slaughter, for tolerating my many questions and interruptions cheerfully; Darwin Bayston, Cathy Kittell, Bob Luck, and their staffs, for making my research easier; and Susan Brennan, for the judicious editing that made my text smoother. Special thanks are due Joni

Tomal, who more than anyone else aided me in the task of making sense of thirty years' worth of sometimes mildewed files.

The generous support of the Institute's staff is the logical consequence of the enthusiasm engendered for this history by Pete Morley, who has been an unflagging partisan of the project from the beginning. Pete literally made the Institute available to me—officers, committees, staff, and files—and then left me to do my work unhampered. Best of all, he gave me Ed Mennis for an editor. Ed has been an unmatched source of information about the Institute. He has tolerated my insufficiencies as a writer and researcher, and through his acute yet considerate editing helped me grow better as both. Ed is not responsible for any errors I may have made, but he is certainly due credit for the accuracy this history has attained. One of the real pleasures of the time spent on this book has been working with Ed Mennis and Pete Morley.

Finally, let me say plainly that I could never have completed this history without the cooperation of my husband, Jonathon Kates, who bears a special relation to the book. A talented writer and keen editor, Jon was first offered the project but turned it down in favor of me. He has been my first and best reader, giving me insights that enabled me to produce a much better book than I could ever have done on my own. For his weekend babysitting and loving, generous support, I am more grateful than I can ever say.

Nancy Regan
Charlottesville, Virginia
January 19, 1987

PART ONE

PREHISTORY

" . . . the birth of the Chartered Financial Analyst designation is itself a tribute to the great improvement in the professional training and attitudes of financial analysts in the past two decades."

Benjamin Graham, 1965

CHAPTER ONE
Should Security Analysts Have a Professional Rating?

In early May 1963, *The Wall Street Journal* told members of the financial community to expect near-record level peacetime profits for American corporations in the second quarter, speculated about the likely political consequences of Nelson Rockefeller's remarriage, and announced the existence of a new examination for security analysts. Though featured on the front page, this last item was hardly "news" to the country's senior analysts. Some 300 of these analysts, in the midst of that spring's resurgent economy and active market, studied for the June 15th examination that would earn them the newly-minted designation, Chartered Financial Analyst.

The real news was that all those who studied for this exam were at least 45 years old—33 of them were over 60—and many had 30 or more years of experience as analysts. The *Journal* found a representative example in Lucien O. Hooper, a senior analyst at W. E. Hutton & Co. In May 1963, Hooper was 66 years old, had 44 years of experience as an analyst (half of them with Hutton), and wrote a regular column for *Forbes*. Moreover, Hooper was a past president of both the New York Society of Security Analysts and the National Federation of Financial Analysts' Societies (which later became the Financial Analysts Federation). Yet he was studying intently for this test. Hooper suggested to the *Journal*'s reporter that he expected the test to be as difficult as a bar exam. In an autobiography published 10 years later, Hooper acknowledged the trepidation with which he and his prominent counterparts approached their task:

> Experienced analysts, like myself, Ragnar Naess, and Joe Galanis, when we took the first exam . . . were really scared that we would not pass. We studied and attended seminars. . . .

Why would such distinguished men as Hooper and his peers risk failing a test on the very subject that had earned them a successful living for a quarter century?

The answers to this improbable question were no doubt as diverse as the 300 analysts themselves, but for most it was a matter of pride: pride in their work and in the growth of their profession. Analysts—whose forerunners were statisticians, complete with green eyeshades, closeted in the back rooms of brokerage houses—had achieved by mid-century a position of considerable prominence and responsibility. David G. Watterson, founding member of the Cleveland Society of Security Analysts recalls that by 1950 "you didn't need to know somebody who knew somebody who knew the president of many of our leading national corporations to get him interested in speaking to the Cleveland Society. He was already interested." Those who had banded together in 1947 to affiliate the various local analyst groups into the National Federation of Financial Analyst Societies saw in their enlarging position within the financial community both a duty and an opportunity to codify and raise the standards of their practice. At the Federation's founding, George Hansen of the Boston Society declared that "were certain fundamental standards set up, whether through examination or establishment of a specified degree, the general quality of workmanship of the analyst would markedly improve. . . . " No one could ever guarantee that an analyst's recommendations would bring riches to an investor, but one could, through the establishment and testing of standards, ensure that analysts making recommendations were qualified to do so.

Despite the commitment of the Federation's early leaders to the idea of testing technical competence, it would be nearly 20 before an analyst hung a charter on the wall. Substantial opposition to testing would be forthcoming, particularly among "sell-side" analysts, who might have much to lose should chartering become standard practice. Others would be offended at the mere suggestion that individuals of their preeminence pass a test, wanting instead, in the words of David Watterson, to be "'blanketed in' without any examination requirement." It was therefore remarkable, when chartering examinations finally became a reality in the spring of 1963, to have over three hundred registrations from the country's best and most experienced analysts. For the 20 years prior to its initial administration, it seemed unlikely that anyone with so much experience and expertise would condescend to take such a test at all.

*   *   *

In 1942, the New York Society of Security Analysts, then five years old, proposed to its members the establishment of a professional rating, tentatively called "Qualified Security Analyst," or QSA. To implement this rating, the Society would set up a "Board of Qualifiers" to confer the title of QSA upon those applicants who met certain "designated standards," including character, education, experience, and the "passing of an examination." The idea for such a rating originated with Benjamin Graham, the acknowledged dean of financial analysis, and was championed by him consistently for the next decade and more. By a margin of 90 to 6, the 1945 NYSSA voted "in principle" for the establishment of such a rating scheme. Yet despite its overwhelming approval (over the vocal dissent, it should be noted, of a certain New York Society member named Lucien Hooper), the QSA plan was not implemented.

Although the proposed rating scheme did not advance far beyond its initial endorsement by the NYSSA in 1942, Graham's idea for the professionalization of the practice of security analysis was sufficiently imaginative and forward-thinking to last through refinement and reworking in the succeeding 20 years.

The first public discussion of the idea of analyst certification appeared in the premiere issue of *The Analyst's Journal*, published by the New York Society in January 1945. There, two eminently worthy opponents debated the question of whether security analysts should have a professional rating. In making the case for the affirmative, Ben Graham outlined a number of advantages: the QSA designation would indicate to the investing public the attainment of certain minimum requirements regarding knowledge and professional competence; for the analyst himself it had the obvious advantage of additional prestige, improved employability, and the possibility of increased financial reward. Furthermore, Graham asserted, the analyst in possession of a QSA would likely develop a keener interest in his work and a more professional attitude. Despite these benefits, Graham saw a lingering issue still unresolved: "The crux of the question," he wrote, "is whether security analysis as a calling has enough of the professional attribute to justify the requirement that its practitioners present to the public evidence of fitness for their work."

Countering Graham's proposal with a negative case was Lucien Hooper. Whatever merits the QSA idea may have had, Hooper argued, there was no particular enthusiasm for ratings either within the analysts' community at large, among their employers, or among "the investors the public serves." Indifference among the society's membership was particularly important because the success of such a self-administered and self-regulated plan, according to Hooper, would depend on "its general acceptance and on the profession's enthusiastic determination to make it work." Moreover, he contended, the analyst's profession had grown and progressed phenomenally in the preceding 25 years without serious abuses, without regimentation, and without the QSA designation. The rating itself, which would be meaningless without enforceable penalties, would require the expenditure of considerable money and the time of "our most competent and busiest members." Hooper wondered also whether the mid 1940s—with much of the younger membership away at war—was a propitious time to implement a rating that would, after all, ultimately mean more to these young analysts than to established senior analysts. Finally, he argued, to institute a rating which, among other things, certified adherence to ethical standards was entirely premature until a code of ethics for analysts had been firmly established.

Hooper's arguments evidently represented the thinking of many analysts at the time, since the certification program did not come about for another 18 years. Yet as Hooper himself noted in his memoirs, Graham's notion of establishing and testing analytical standards was "a good idea." Unfortunately, it was premature. "The profession was not ready for it," Hooper recalled, "and it had not been thought through." However, the "thinking through" phase certainly had begun. By July 1945, the NYSSA had formulated and published the Code of Ethics that Hooper had called for. Furthermore, discussions concerning the desirability of certifying security analysts continued to appear in *The Analyst's Journal* throughout the late 1940s. Often these articles were authored by Ben Graham, writing under his own name or as "Cogitator." Reports from the Committee on Standards, which he headed for several years, also were issued. At the same time, individual societies—among them Boston, New York and San Francisco—were developing courses of instruction for junior analysts, often in cooperation with local universities. In 1947, the New York Society, of which Graham was a member, allied itself with analysts' groups from Boston, Chicago, Philadelphia, and Providence to found the National Federation of Financial Analysts Societies. This provided the certification issue its necessary national audience.

By 1951, the NFFAS's Committee on Professional Ethics and Standards, under the chairmanship of Ragnar D. Naess of New York, had assumed the burden of carrying out further studies among the Federation's membership concerning the feasibility of instituting a certification program. While the members as a whole seemed to have a "definite awareness of the need for establishing higher professional standards," Naess reported, there still was "some difference of opinion in New York as to whether this should be done at all, and as to what method should be followed if it is done." Past NYSSA presidents Lucien O. Hooper and N. Leonard Jarvis, among others, remained skeptical about the merits of such a rating. The New York Society was, however, deeply involved in composing a program of its own to certify security analysts as CSAs (Chartered Security Analysts). Walter K. Gutman, the chairman of the NYSSA's Standards and Ethics Committee, had submitted a proposal for such a program, sent a questionnaire to his Society's members about it, and received a "very high" number of favorable responses.

To determine the National Federation's view of such a program, Naess's committee discussed it among themselves and circulated it to the presidents of the constituent societies. If anything, the executives of these Societies felt that the New York proposal was a little too undemanding. George Hansen of Boston found the New York tests "rather on the 'considerate' side." Others concurred. The most universally held opinion revealed by this early discussion, however, was not that the tests were too simple but that their intended audience was too small. "If the degree [of CSA] is to have any meaning," one committee member wrote, "the program should be administered on a national basis. . . . " A society president had much the same idea: "The value of any such program is greatly reduced if done on an individual Society basis . . . the only way to handle it is to have the National Federation's [Professional Ethics and Standards] Committee pick up these recommendations. . . . " So it did, indicating in its 1952 report that "a program be carried forward that will accomplish the aim as outlined by the executive committee of the New York Society. . . . " Though formulating such a program admittedly would be difficult, the committee believed that it was "highly desirable that a great deal of attention should be given to this problem on a national rather than a sectional basis."

*   *   *

The history of the development of a program for certifying financial analysts is a record of continual, small refinements in Benjamin Graham's broad idea. By 1952, some 10 years after Graham first raised the issue to the fledgling New York Society, the analyst community had accepted in principle the idea that their members should have some kind of certification program, national in scope. The next question—to be answered through these small, incremental refinements—would be what form the program should take. The final step would be to convince the senior members that the program was acceptable—not just "in principle" for the younger members, but in *fact*, for themselves as well.

As Ragnar Naess's committee had hoped, the chartering of analysts soon received great attention. In 1953, Shelby Cullom Davis, also of the New York Society, chaired a Professional Ethics and Standards subcommittee specifically to review a proposal circulating around the New York Society to set up a classification of "Senior Security Analyst." To receive such a designation, a NYSSA member would have to attest to having at least 10 years of experience in security analysis and responsibilities associated with a senior position. He also would have to submit to a "board of examiners" at least one analytical study appraising securities and written within five years of applying. The board of examiners would themselves be "Senior Security Analysts, NYSSA"—although how they would achieve that designation was not clear.

Davis's subcommittee found that members of other societies questioned the "advisability" of the 10 year requirement and preferred to see greater emphasis placed on knowledge and standards, which could be tested. One analyst feared that rewarding duration would be akin to "the position taken by many of our trade unions that seniority . . . be the sole or primary determination of anyone's qualifications." As a possible correction to an undue emphasis on the length of one's experience, Davis's committee cited the program of certification undergone by Chartered Life Underwriters. In addition to meeting age, character, educational, and experience criteria, applicants for CLUs had to pass four-hour written examinations in five required fields, judged by life insurance representatives and educators. In the long run, the subcommittee concluded, such an examination program (closer in fact to Graham's idea) might be needed to attain "a professional status for security analysis," and if so, "it should be done by the leading security analysts of the United States acting jointly with leading educators in business and finance. . . . "

If, as the committee noted, such a program could not exist "unless there [were] more of a universal demand for professional status" than was apparent among Federation members, then the core of Federation leaders interested in certification needed to come up with a concrete, attractive alternative to the proposals thus far advanced by the New York Society. The first such alternative surfaced in mid-1953 when the University of Chicago's School of Business drafted a tentative program for analyst certification. The proposal was circulated by committee member William C. Norby of Chicago, later a Federation president. He and fellow Chicagoans, M. Dutton Morehouse and J. Parker Hall, had met with the Business School dean and several faculty members to discuss the possibility of a certification program and an annual seminar. The Chicago School's "Tentative Proposal" provided for systematic testing of analysts, through a three-stage series of eight examinations. These examinations would initially be composed and graded by the School of Business at Chicago, eventually becoming the purview of a "Committee on Education and Examinations" from within the National Federation.

By early June, the Chicago proposal was making the rounds of the Professional Ethics and Standards Committee, and being read by the Federation's officers, Samuel Jones of Philadelphia, Dutton Morehouse, and Boston's George Hansen. In a detailed series of letters circulating between early June and late September, the committee members expressed their dissatisfaction. Virtually everyone found the proposal "too bookish," leaning as it did on academic topics for its proposed eight exams. Committee members knew only too well that successful investment analysis depended on a good deal more than financial and economic theories. Without experience, one could, in the words of William Held of the San Francisco Society, "complete all eight parts of the proposed course and wind up like James I of England—the wisest fool in Christendom." Likewise objectionable to many of the committee members was the provision to exempt "some members of senior standing" from Associateship and Preliminary examinations and to grant "honorary Fellowship [i.e., CSA degrees] to a senior and select group within the present membership." N. Leonard Jarvis of New York, long an opponent to *any* certification plan, criticized this idea: "What an immediate bonanza to the few exempt favorites [who] could, with benign amusement, look down upon the hundreds of their co-members who would have to go through the nuisance and ordeal of the three sets of examinations." Such a situation, Jarvis feared, would turn the alliance of independent societies that comprised the NFFAS into an "undemocratic oligarchy." In a similar manner, William Held worried that the reaction among analysts to such an exemption would be,"why work along with the bookworms for a Fellowship when you can be a big political noise in the Federation and get an honorary award?"

The fundamental issues thwarting further development of a certification program for analysts were expressed by the members of the 1953 Standards Committee in their testy and somewhat confused correspondence that summer. Assuming that the lack of widespread support for certification could be overcome and that analysts could be made to see that certification, as William Norby expressed it, was not for "personal aggrandizement" but rather to give their work the "mental discipline . . . required to achieve professionalism," what would be the subject matter of this discipline? In addition, there was the question of who would compose and administer tests on the required knowledge, and who would be exempt from these tests? Should the field be defined by the academic community, as represented by the University of Chicago, or could analysts themselves agree upon what to know and who to test? Could senior analysts with years of experience realistically be expected to take tests? Yet should they be exempt? Their participation would lend analyst certification desirability and prestige—but would they participate? Confronted with these thorny issues, the committee retreated: what could not be resolved should be studied further. With the vote on certification split 5-5, the committee reported to the Federation's officers that certification should be a "long-term" rather than an intermediate aim. A subcommittee should be appointed to explore definite procedures, and, as the Federation secretary George Hansen recorded, a Mr. A. Moyer "Abe" Kulp of Philadelphia "might well be chosen as chairman of the subcommittee" because he was "generally favorably inclined toward the accepted plan. . . . "

*   *   *

Perhaps all good ideas become good not because of their inherent worth, as Plato would have it, but rather because of who takes them up. Truth, according to the American pragmatist William James, the grandson of a merchant and banker, is what *happens* to an idea. What happened to Benjamin Graham's "good idea" was that it became embodied in the person of Abe Kulp of Philadelphia. Appointed to the Professional Ethics and Standards Committee by Ragnar Naess in 1950, Kulp chaired the committee in 1952, guided the 1954 program subcommittee, and in 1955 again assumed the chairmanship of the full committee. He held this position until the creation of the Institute of Chartered Financial Analysts and became its first president. Perhaps more than others who studied the idea before him, Abe Kulp was a partisan of analyst certification. As long-time committee member Ragnar Naess remembers, Kulp "felt that the integrity of financial analysts was of prime importance and that the confidence in Wall Street and in the honesty and ability of financial institutions would be greatly enhanced" through a professional rating. Though wise enough and sufficiently patient to push the program through no faster than the Federation membership could accept it, Kulp was nonetheless persistent in his belief that analysts *should* acquire a professional rating. The question for him was not whether, but when.

Yet if timing was crucial, so was method. The University of Chicago's "Tentative Proposal for the Certification of Security Analysts" continued to be the educational program used as a model by Kulp's committee. But as early as 1955 they had begun to modify its suggested administration. Rather than have a university oversee certification, Kulp's committee proposed that it would be preferable to have "an independent organization of stature administer the program if it is to command the respect and support of the various segments in the financial and investment fields." To be patterned after the American Institute for Property and Casualty Underwriters, such an agency might be called

"American Institute of Financial Analysis and Investment Management," and because of its wider scope would award a designation somewhat broader than Chartered Security Analyst.

Hoping for a favorable response (again, "in principle") from the Federation's directors, Kulp's committee even submitted a procedure for setting up the so-called "American Institute" and means of financing it via federation grants, investment community contributions, and candidate fees, with the idea that the "complete setup . . . would be in operation by the fall of 1956." They were congratulated for their thoroughness by Federation president Dutton Morehouse, who called their report "the best ever submitted at an annual meeting." Nevertheless, Kulp's committee did not receive an endorsement. The Federation directors felt it would be "unwise" to proceed with implementation. Instead they asked the subcommittee on certification to prepare a report for the 1956 Directors' Meeting "setting forth specific recommendations."

Despite its eagerness and specificity, the 1955 report failed to provide solutions to the major problems impeding creation of an institute. No code of ethics yet existed for the Federation, and a standard body of knowledge had not been devised. Security analysts performed many diverse functions for their employers, who were themselves a varied group: stock brokers, investment bankers, life insurance companies, pension and endowment funds, financial corporations, and so forth. An analyst might be primarily a statistician, or might manage a multi-million dollar pension fund, depending upon his field of employment. Given this variability, what did one need to know to be certified as a security analyst? The answer to this question would require constant revision, long after the establishment of a rating program; but until some definition of a standard body of knowledge had been offered, no program could exist.

Although the committee itself had not proposed a body of knowledge other than the examination contents of the 1953 University of Chicago proposal, the NFFAS took a step toward clarifying what analysts needed to know. Through the efforts of William C. Norby and Dutton Morehouse, both of the Chicago Society, the Federation began a series of annual summer seminars in August 1956. Administered by Professor Marshall Ketchum of the University of Chicago, the seminars were held at Beloit College in Wisconsin, and brought the country's leading analysts together to discuss issues facing their profession.

Standards of knowledge would begin to take shape within the seminars and through the committee's work, but the problem of exemptions for older, established analysts stubbornly resisted solution. The stated purpose of a certification program was "to establish sound and adequate professional standards." Would a certification program — even though voluntary — command respect if exemptions were given? The 1955 and 1956 reports failed to handle this problem constructively. Although the consensus of the committee was that a "grandfather clause would be undesirable," it left the matter for "further objective study," rather than reaching a potentially binding conclusion.

Because such crucial issues remained unresolved, action on the certification of analysts languished for several years. The Professional Ethics and Standards Committee continued to wrestle with the problems that accompanied a long-range program, but its reports shrank from the assertive four-page program of 1955 to a diffident three paragraphs in 1957. Indeed, as Federation President Robert J. Wilkes morosely acknowledged to the membership that year, "It may appear that progress has been slow, and it is true that we do not have many tangible developments to show for all the work that has been done."

Appearances were deceiving. Despite its progressively laconic reports, the Professional Ethics and Standards Committee, primarily in the person of Abe Kulp, had been slowly amassing new ideas and new evidence in favor of certification. In the summer of 1957 Kulp had contacted Willis Winn, vice dean of the Wharton School, to solicit his ideas for an analyst program. Winn responded at length in July, citing his experience with the Chartered Life Underwriters and their education and certification problems. While not providing a concrete program, as the University of Chicago had in 1953, Winn did discuss in detail probable topics for study and testing. Moreover, he supplied the committee with needed moral support in its difficult decision about the grandfather clause. Acknowledging the need for uniformly high standards in setting up a certification program, Winn maintained that such standards "can be maintained only if all those receiving the professional recognition be required to go over the same hurdles." He continued:

> As you know, the C.L.U. people have been fighting the "grandfather clause" for years and are finally convinced that the action they have taken is a proper one. . . . [I]t would be a great mistake to undertake such a program as you envisage if you are confronted with the necessity of including a number of very capable practitioners and professional people on the basis of their position.

After years of hearing negative rumblings, Kulp must have welcomed such experienced reassurance.

Early in 1958, Federation president Gilbert Palmer of Cleveland gave the certification issue some much-needed publicity. In a presidential newsletter detailing his visits with several societies, Palmer described his discussions about the possibility of certifying analysts. Noting that there had not been "much motion towards certification in the past three years" except Abe Kulp's "conversations with experts," Palmer cleared the way for later progress by responding to some objections and misapprehensions that arose during his travels. Analysis was an art—or at best "a very immature science," he told his questioners—but it could, like medicine, still be explored. Yes, veteran analysts would probably have to study diligently—but "would this be bad?" Yes, most "certified analysts" would be young men—but then this was designed to be a "long-range" program. No, certification would *not* be a requirement, merely voluntary.

While Palmer spread the word to Federation members, Kulp circulated a revision of the 1955 certification proposal among his committee, the Federation's Executive Committee, and some Philadelphia Society officers. The proposal was accompanied by a questionnaire on the status of the professionalization movement and on "grandfathering." Their replies were uniformly in favor of the proposal and against the idea of exemptions. Grandfathering, one P.E.S. Committee member wrote, "would cast some cloud on the whole program"; another feared that exemptions might let into the program those "whose qualifications and abilities were mediocre." One Philadelphia Society member concluded, bravely: "I think we should go ahead, knowing I probably wouldn't pass." Support was finally growing.

By the time the Federation met in Los Angeles in May 1958, its directors were ready for a full-scale debate on a most specific program. Based largely on its 1955 report, and incorporating, as that one did, the University of Chicago's 1953 "Tentative Proposal," Kulp's committee submitted to the directors another concrete framework for certifying analysts. Notably new in this report and its amendments were the recognition that no Institute could be a reality without "the selection of a suitable man to head" it and a request that the Federation directors, in the words of Abe Kulp, "authorize your committee to conduct an investigation into the selection of a suitable high-caliber educational institution which would be interested in undertaking [such] a program . . . [and] would conduct the examinations, supervising and cooperating with other educational institutions, to set up the desired courses of study in various sections of the country." Thus, although an "American Institute of Financial Analysis and Investment Management" was once again propounded, the actual composition and administration of tests would be through a highly regarded university.

Despite nine years of intensive committee work on certification and nine years of annual reports annually approved, and despite the presentation of a long-requested concrete proposal, the Federation directors balked. Perhaps they were made uneasy by the new committee's attitude toward exemptions: the 1958 report clearly stated that a "grandfather clause would be undesirable and would threaten the general acceptance of this whole proposal"—without the usual proviso for "further study" of the matter. Perhaps, as one board member suggested, certification was "a relatively new subject" to those who had been directors for fewer than three years. Outgoing President Gilbert Palmer of Cleveland saw it differently: "Actually, we have, over quite a number of years, approved a step to certification as a body. We

-15-

have approved Abe Kulp's committee reports. There is no point to this committee report if we don't approve certification."

One who had lived with the question of certification longer than anyone present, including Abe Kulp, was Federation past president Lucien O. Hooper. After listening to these exchanges and other seemingly nervous debates about what kind of examination might be generated and whether it would favor "younger and younger men with more knowledge of details," Hooper spoke out in support of Kulp's proposal. Suggesting that it would be "extremely unfortunate to ask Abe Kulp to go ahead without a strong endorsement by the Federation . . . so that he can negotiate with an institution with the feeling that something may really come of it," Hooper recommended that Kulp's report be accepted "in general principle" and that "a definite appropriation of money" be made. The directors were less hardy than Mr. Hooper; they voted not to give Abe Kulp authority to set up a definite certification program with an educational program. Instead, as outgoing President Palmer noted, they "approved the *idea* of certification, as they have in the past, but not the *deed.*"

With the directors' endorsement, however weak, the process of accreditation continued. The new Federation executive vice president, A. Hamilton Bolton of Toronto, contacted the University of Chicago, source of the earlier program. Bolton, along with Federation members Dutton Morehouse and William Norby, met with Chicago Business School dean Alan Wallace and Professor Marshall Ketchum to set up a *modus operandi* for certification. It was agreed that the likely person to construct this was Professor Ezra Solomon, who had worked on Chicago's 1953 proposal. By late August 1958 the University had submitted a budget for the work. By October Professor Solomon had received his first payment and a certification program for security analysts was in its final stage of development.

*   *   *

The Solomon Proposal was ready in mid-March 1959. It was the intention of Committee Chairman Kulp and Federation president L. Hartley Smith to bring Professor Solomon's ideas before the Federation's Executive Committee at its April meeting.

To facilitate discussion at the meeting, Kulp mailed a copy of the formal proposal to each Executive Committee member and to those on his own committee on March 26.

Solomon's work made an immediate, favorable impact on the Ethics and Standards group. One member called it "a major forward step"; others recognized that their long labors towards passing a certification program might finally bear fruit. Once the Proposal had been passed on by the Executive Committee, the Professional Ethics and Standards Committee was to work with the University of Chicago on any necessary revisions, and then submit the finalized version to all Federation directors. The hope, according to President Smith, was "to allow an adequate opportunity for discussion within each individual society. . . . " To become accepted, this voluntary certification program would have to be passed by a majority of the directors. Even at this late date, some members still resisted the idea of certification. The existence of one more proposal, however specific and judicious, was not likely to interest them.

If the new Solomon Proposal was not guaranteed universal acceptance, however, it was certainly assured careful perusal. More than anything submitted earlier, this was a concrete, workable plan for the creation of an Institute to administer examinations and oversee the professionalization of financial analysis. Solomon's proposal was supplemented with a tentative curriculum that included suggested readings and contained several features previously unconsidered. First, the proposal provided for a group, to be culled from within the Federation, to organize the suggested certification program and elect administrative officers. This "Initiating Group" would be composed of Federation members who qualified for the exams (as provided in the document) and who had "published two or more professional papers in *The Analyst's Journal* prior to December 28, 1958." Solomon estimated that this would involve between 65 and 75 members, depending on whether or not Federation membership prior to 1952 became a requirement for candidacy as stipulated. Although this method of selecting an "Initiating Group" would, as Solomon acknowledged, omit "a significant number of people who have been extremely active in the

accreditation and education movement and in NFFAS in general,"
he nevertheless felt it might be the "*least* arbitrary" method of
composing such a group. Moreover, he believed it would provide
an initiating group of the right size: "small enough to avoid the
'stigma' of a 'self-selected' group of 'grandfathers' and big enough
to provide the energy and points of view needed in the first year
committees."

Solomon was willing to tackle the "grandfather" problem in a
new way as well. Wishing neither to admit them all without
examination, nor to require them to take all three examinations at
a time when most were policy-makers and managers, "no longer
engaged in day-to-day work involving" financial accounting,
statistics, or individual security analysis, Solomon effected a
compromise. Federation members born prior to December 31,
1914, would be required to take only the third examination.
Members born prior to December 31, 1924, could omit the first.
(There would be time limits on this partial exemption, of course.)
According to Solomon's new scheme, everyone wishing to attain
accreditation would be examined, but not on areas where
experience obviated need.

Besides forming an Initiating Group and presenting a solution
to the "grandfather" issue, Solomon's 1959 proposal added some
familiar phrases to the typical analyst's vocabulary. "The
NFFAS," he wrote, "should establish an Institute of Chartered
Financial Analysts." As members, analysts would be entitled to
use the "professional designation of *Chartered Financial Analyst* to
be indicated by the letters C.F.A. after a person's name." After all
the years of "QSAs", "CSAs", "fellows", and "associates,"
Solomon argued that only the designation Chartered Financial
Analyst made sufficient sense. It bespoke both "professional
status" and "ongoing professional standards," while avoiding the
implication of either "once-and-for-all" certification or that
membership in the Institute constituted some kind of "license."

Finally, the proposal provided a detailed curriculum for the
three examinations leading to attainment of the CFA designation.
Solomon believed that the profession was better served by
tailoring the curriculum to parallel an analyst's actual career
rather than university courses. Reasoning that an analyst first

learns the basic tools of his trade, then acts in a staff capacity, and finally moves on to decision- and policy-making, Solomon designed the examinations in a manner that would "encourage and guide people to make a systematic study of subject matter areas which tie in with their work. . . . " Thus, the newer analysts taking Part One would be examined on financial accounting, statistics, the American economy and its variables, and the instruments and institutions of securities markets. Those taking Part Two would be tested on economic growth and fluctuations, and industry, regional, financial, and specific security analysis. Analysts proceeding to Part Three would be required to demonstrate their competence as decision-makers and their ability to determine investment goals, balance portfolios, and select industries and securities; they also would be tested on their knowledge of time purchases and sales. All candidates would answer and be graded anonymously; all would be examined "on the same day throughout the country."

Abe Kulp and his committee had been waiting a long time for a workable proposal; at last they had it. Kulp brought the proposal before the Federation's Executive Committee on April 10, 1959, and received their unanimous consent to proceed, with a few revisions. The Executive Committee concluded that the proposed Initiating Group was impractical, as there was no assurance that it would "be made up of individuals who were senior analysts and who could be depended upon to take an active part in forwarding Accreditation." This concern led them to stipulate that the Initiating Group be composed of "past presidents of the member Societies who were still practicing analysts."

Subsequent revisions were forthcoming, but the committee gave Abe Kulp their approval to mail a copy of Solomon's complete proposal to all members of the 22 constituent societies (approximately six thousand people). The mailing would include a questionnaire to determine whether individual members were in agreement with the "principle of Accreditation" and whether they would take the "necessary steps to become accredited" themselves. For the first time, the entire Federation membership would have the opportunity to examine and comment on a specific accreditation proposal. The results of Kulp's survey became available on June 12 and were presented to the Federation's directors at the Montreal meeting on the 14th. The directors' judgment at that meeting ultimately would determine the Institute's fate.

Kulp's presentation seemed ill-fated from the beginning. Copies of the the lauded Solomon proposal had been improperly collated, rendering it incomprehensible. In addition, however thorough Professor Solomon had been in suggesting a *modus operandi* for an Institute, he had neglected to take into account the different problems facing Canadian Federation members. This was particularly unfortunate since the director's meeting was being held in Montreal, home city of the incoming Federation president. Although Kulp's certification questionnaire had "a large favorable response," in Montreal and Toronto, he reported with obvious chagrin that about half of those responding had said: "How about Canada—do we have to take exactly the same examination?" Kulp quickly apologized for the "oversight."

There were other problems that required attention. The report had "unintentionally" been condensed in certain areas, resulting in the misconception that the Initiating Group would automatically become Institute members without the requirement of even one examination. This was hardly what the committee wanted to convey, as the "grandfather" issue had delayed accreditation for so long. Moreover, there was considerable misunderstanding about how the creation of an Institute would affect the Federation. Some members believed that if such a plan went through, one "wouldn't be a member of the financial analysts society any more." Since many of the directors present did not intend to take the examination, the Professional Ethics and Standards Committee certainly did not want to imply that their memberships would be terminated.

Perhaps more disconcerting was the directors' disagreement over statistical interpretations. Citing both the results of Kulp's questionnaire on accreditation and Sheldon Gordon's statistical work among Federation members, done for a Wharton School master's thesis, the directors disagreed strongly over whether a majority of support for accreditation existed. Kulp's results showed 74 percent in favor and 26 percent against. Gordon's more scientifically random poll of analysts revealed 61 percent in favor, 24.8 percent opposed and 14 percent undecided. Could the directors accept the suggestion—which Kulp acknowledged was not yet proven—that the 14 percent undecided at the time of Gordon's poll had shifted to approval upon seeing the revised Solomon proposal? Or should they instead conclude, as one director argued, that because only 20 percent of the total membership responded to Kulp's questionnaire, nearly 80 percent should be viewed as either "uninterested or opposed" to the program for accreditation?

To help resolve the dispute, past President Dutton Morehouse noted that a 20 percent response from Federation members should not be interpreted as indicative of no interest, because in his many years of surveying analysts, "the hardest thing that I have ever tried to do is to get an expression of opinion out of this group of people. They just plain won't answer mail. . . . " To Morehouse, the opposing directors were "completely unjustified" in trying to assert that a proportionately small response meant that "the other people are all against" accreditation. The efficient handling of the "grandfather" issue, the setting of high minimum standards, and the diversity of Solomon's proposed curriculum all spoke more eloquently, in Morehouse's opinion, in favor of accreditation than statistical interpretations argued against.

For years, President Smith recalled, "all previous directors meetings had discussed this thing only in matters of very general terms." Now, finally, "competent" educators had come up with something tangible. The now familiar anticertification arguments which continued even among the directors must have been disheartening to Smith, Morehouse, Kulp and others who had answered them again and again. However, Solomon's "tangible" proposal was not without effect. During the discussion of it, an important shift took place. Nathan Bowen, past president of the New York Society—long the locus of much anticertification sentiment—was expected to oppose Kulp's report. Instead he came out in favor of it:

Before I came here, I had decided to vote against this. The comments here have been quite interesting. I'm just too old, and I think there are a few others, right around me in this room—and certainly in the Societies—that are not interested enough to take any examinations. However, I do think that the program outlined by Abe's committee is a good one and it will mean a lot . . . to the younger analysts coming along—boys in college and the fellows coming out. I think I'll vote for it.

George Hansen remembers Bowen's support as the "back-breaker" of the opposition. President Smith thanked Bowen and put Kulp's report to a vote. Upon the insistence of Lawrence Kahn of New York, who noted the historic importance of voting on "something that's been up before this Board for many years," Secretary George Hansen called the roll. The dissenters, it turned out, were a decided, if vocal, minority: the motion to accept and implement Kulp's committee report on the Solomon proposal carried, 56 to 13. For Abe Kulp, who had lived with the idea of certification longer and more intimately than anyone, it was "a very sobering, as well as a very happy moment. . . . " To those who had as vigorously opposed the movement as he had championed it, Kulp gave a promise to seek "their cooperation and advice," so that the new Institute "will not be a divisive movement in any way."

*   *   *

When Abe Kulp announced in the next issue of *The Analyst's Journal* (July 1959) that the "Directors of the National Federation of Financial Analysts Societies made history at the Montreal Convention," he wasn't exaggerating. In approving the report of the Professional Ethics and Standards Committee for Analyst Accreditation and in establishing the proposed Institute of Chartered Financial Analysts, they managed to make professionalization of the practice of financial analysis a realistic goal.

Why did accreditation finally pass after so many years of talk? Perhaps just because there *had* been so many years. Although a few of the 1959 directors professed relative unfamiliarity with the idea of certification, most of these 69 men had lived with the idea for the better part of a decade. Familiarity, in this case, bred not contempt but acceptance. *Whether they wanted it for themselves or not,* the Federation directors had come to recognize that the profession as a whole needed to acquire a means of matching its growing responsibility with high standards of knowledge and ethical behavior.

Moreover, the Federation itself had, by 1959, attained sufficient strength as an organization to address itself to philosophical issues facing the profession. From a loose organization of five analyst societies in 1947, the Federation had expanded exponentially. As 1952 Federation president Richard Lambourne recalls, the young Federation experienced an "eruption of growth" in the 1950s. The Federation's founding purpose was to "promote the welfare of the profession" and from its earliest days it had committees to oversee "education and training" and "ethics and standards." However, the simple fact was that for its first decade the National Federation of Financial Analyst Societies had to concentrate on balancing the needs of a loose and sometimes disparate group of regional societies. Certification—or chartering—was a national issue, not a local one. Until the Federation had a firm identity, it could not rise above regional conflicts to address national, professional concerns.

Furthermore, even as its strength consolidated, its membership began to change. By 1959, a demographic swing in the analyst population had begun. Since few men and women entered the profession between the start of the Depression and the start of World War II, most analysts practising at the Federation's founding had become statisticians and then analysts before 1929. But the end of the War—with its returning, eager veterans and their G. I. Bill educations—and an expanding economy produced a gradual but profound shift in the average age of analysts. By the time Ezra Solomon published his proposal in 1959, he estimated that nearly half of the Federation membership had joined after 1952. Many of these newer members, moreover, had been born after 1924. The Federation, thus, was becoming filled with "younger and younger" men and women whose knowledge of "all those details" had worried some older policy makers at the Los Angeles meeting. Those new members also were those to whom possession of a CFA might be a matter not only of pride and professionalism, but also advancement.

But more than population shifts and Federation strength, the credit for the final passage of analyst accreditation goes to the senior analysts who were willing to put their prestige on the line for the benefit of the profession. After years of struggling with the "grandfather" issue, after years of hearing from people who, in the words of Federation and later Institute President David D. Williams "weren't about to spend nine hours writing an exam with uncertain results," the older analysts agreed to be tested. Possible (if not likely) failure was not the only issue, however. From the senior analyst's viewpoint the establishment of a CFA institute might also have an undesirable leveling effect. As early as 1952, Federation President Dick Lambourne had written to Shelby Cullom Davis that "many of the older security analysts take the view that awarding a professional rating to younger men might have an equalizing effect. . . . [T]he years of experience put in by older men could be minimized by the advent of much younger men who hold the same professional 'degree'." Lambourne warned in that letter that this potential leveling should not stand in the way. In Montreal, seven years later, the Federation directors in effect agreed. They, and subsequently the entire Federation membership, put the welfare of the profession ahead of self-interest.

Thus, it was no overstatement on Abe Kulp's part to note the significance of the June 14, 1959, directors meeting. When the Federation directors voted then to establish an Institute of Chartered Financial Analysts, they affected their profession permanently.

PART TWO

THE ORGANIZING YEARS

*We started on the mezzanine at Monroe
Hall and I had one gal, Nancy
Anderson—that was my staff. George
Hansen gave me one file cabinet and said
"That should last you ten years."*

C. Stewart Sheppard
first executive director of ICFA

CHAPTER TWO
The Search for a Director

"The selection of a director . . . will be a most important step in establishing the Institute on a sound basis and providing the necessary leadership," the *Federation Newsletter* reported in June 1960. Such a position, the article continued, "will require a man of vigor, ability, and stature." In fact, the casualness with which the directorship requirements were stated (anonymously by Abe Kulp) belied what was becoming, an increasingly unpropitious and unproductive search. The final revision of the Solomon proposal had been finished and accepted by the Federation directors in April, the Initiating Group had been formed and would be in place in July. The task that had preoccupied Kulp, however, was nowhere near completion.

The idea of having an independent paid director with "good academic background, satisfactory administrative ability, and outstanding leadership qualities" first surfaced in the 1955 report of Kulp's committee. Kulp's files for the years surrounding the Montreal Convention (1957-61) expand upon the 1955 report and are jammed with notes about the qualities a director of the Institute should have, lists of likely candidates, and lists of people to contact for more lists of more likely candidates.

Though such material is often difficult to date, it appears that as early as mid-1957, Abe Kulp had formulated specific ideas of what to look for in the potential director of the hitherto nonexistent Institute. Such a person, Kulp wrote, should be of an "educational background," should have "stature" in his field and "wide connections in [the] academic and financial world." He "must like people," have "promotional ability," be able to get cooperation from colleges around the country and be available to the proposed Institute—"say 75 percent of the time." Thus, long before the Montreal meeting gave him a director's slot to fill, Abe Kulp had defined for himself and his committee a nearly impossible task: Find an extroverted academic of high standing who was widely-connected in the financial world and who possessed the one thing such a man was least likely to have—a lot of free time.

In his zeal to get the Institute approved, Abe Kulp had to overlook the notable lack of an explicit provision for a director in Ezra Solomon's 1959 proposal. Solomon suggested only that the Institute have annually elected officers and a "full-time paid registrar." Yet, in discussing the mechanics of setting up the Institute via an Initiating Group, Solomon did comment in the pages following his formal proposal that it might be desirable to get "a respected academician—either retired (e.g., Ben Graham) or on leave of absence—to serve for a year as a full-time paid officer of the Institute during its first year of existence." The role of such an officer would be to formulate the examination, explain and promote it to constituent societies, develop curriculum outlines and study guides, and supervise the administration and grading of examinations.

Kulp, of course, recognized the need for formalizing Solomon's off-hand suggestion. One of the two substantive revisions Kulp made in the 1959 Professional Ethics and Standards Committee Report (which incorporated Solomon's proposal) was to spell out unambiguously that the Institute's Executive Council, elected by the Initiating Group, would have the authority to search out and employ a "paid, part-time director" who would become an *ex officio* member of the Executive Council. Together with a restructuring of Solomon's examination procedures which allowed the new Institute more flexibility in setting dates and deadlines, this provision for an administrator constituted Kulp's only major revision agreement. Submitted to the Federation directors in March 1960, these changes were approved on April 30 by an even greater margin than the original report: 68 in favor, none opposed, 9 not voting.

As Kulp's files make clear, however, his search for a director did not await Federation approval. As early as September 1959, he was discussing with the Federation's Executive Committee the likely candidacy of two University of Chicago professors, Marshall Ketchum and Ezra Solomon. Solomon was an obvious choice, of course, given his critical role in composing a framework for the Institute. Ketchum also had much to offer: long connected with the Chicago Society, he had been director of the Analysts Seminar at Beloit since its inception four years earlier. But both men were already heavily committed, within their university and beyond, and neither was in a likely position to take on the considerable challenge of becoming the Institute's first director.

By May 1960 Kulp had sounded out six men who were "logical choices" but no one had been found who was either able or willing to "disengage himself quickly enough" for the task at hand. The name of Benjamin Graham, however, frequently appeared on Kulp's lists from 1960, causing Kulp to write a note to himself to "check Graham again." Graham had retired to Beverly Hills, was teaching part time at UCLA, and was in his own words too distant "from the center of things" to become involved. (In fact, he never chose to earn the charter he had so long advocated.)

It had become abundantly clear by the fall of 1960 that finding the right director was not going to be a simple matter. The Institute's Initiating Group of 159 present and past Society presidents had been in place since July; a nominating committee chaired by Robert J. Wilkes of Boston had solicited names from them and posted a list of candidates for Institute officers on which they had voted. Abe Kulp, who with remarkable modesty had not suggested himself as an officer because he did not "want to push on the basis of 'committee seniority'," had been elected chairman of the new Institute by a vote of 135 to 0. The rest of the Executive Council for the Institute had received the same margin: David D. Williams of Detroit was its vice chairman; Dutton Morehouse of Chicago, its secretary; Gilbert Palmer of Cleveland, E. Linwood

Savage of Boston, Howard Tharsing of San Francisco and Grant Torrance of Kansas City were the councilors. All were to serve until October 31, 1961. George Hansen, the Federation's treasurer, would fill the same role for the Institute. On paper, at least, the Institute of Chartered Financial Analysts existed.

A paper Institute was hardly what Abe Kulp and the other accreditation leaders wanted from their decade-long struggle to professionalize security analysis. The stated purpose of the Institute was to "sponsor and conduct a set of examinations designed to test individual competence and skill in the fields of knowledge pertinent to the professional practice of security analysis." But the Federation leaders—many of whom would sit for the first exam—could not regard themselves as competent to construct such examinations, nor would they be sufficiently disinterested. Moreover, in addition to their heavy commitments to the Federation and the Institute, the members of the Executive Council were men with successful and demanding careers: Kulp was senior vice president at the Wellington Management Company and director of the Wellington Fund, Palmer was vice president of Cleveland National City Bank, Williams vice president and trust officer for the National Bank of Detroit, and so on. As it was, Federation and Institute business was often conducted on weekends. As Lucien Hooper had predicted 15 years earlier, the Institute was eliciting a considerable expenditure of time by the "most competent and busiest analysts." There simply was no more time left to devote to the daily business of administering examinations. Even Abe Kulp, who was notably uncomplaining about the time the Institute demanded, admitted that he had had to give up virtually all of his leisure time to devote himself to Institute matters. At least initially, the Institute's Executive Council needed to employ an academician to run the program.

Kulp had begun his search in the late 1950s by drawing up lists of individual candidates and their qualifications; then, on the Federation's advice, he had written to prominent business schools (notably, Harvard, Columbia, Wharton and Chicago); from these had come more lists of individuals—but no director. The initial canvassing of candidates had not been "productive," and Kulp was no doubt ready—some eighteen months after the Montreal convention—to alter his plan.

The search for an "academic man, young or middle-aged, a vigorous man with . . . ten or fifteen years of active work ahead of him . . . [an] eligible director that can and will do the job" proved stubbornly hard to complete. Meeting with the Federation's Executive Committee in October, Kulp informed them of a slight change in strategy. Rather than continue to pursue particular candidates himself, Kulp had decided to send the deans of a number of leading business schools (in addition to the four already contacted), a "'prospectus' of our requirements of a director"—a kind of selective direct mail approach. The Executive Committee, now increasingly aware of the difficulties Kulp was encountering, suggested two further alternatives. The first involved splitting the directorship between two men, with one being a retired individual who would handle "much of the time consuming detail." The other more widely favored idea was to put the responsibility for administering the CFA program directly into a dean's office, rather than in the hands of an individual, with the detail work apportioned among the dean's staff and graduate students. Proponents of this approach believed that "the prestige of a job coming through a dean's office would also be of considerable value to the Institute in its early years." The school selected could, as Gilbert Palmer wrote to Abe Kulp a few months later, "increase its prestige by doing an outstanding job for us."

In suggesting that Kulp try to put the directorship into a dean's office, the Federation's Executive Committee forced him, in effect, to see things peripherally. Looking too intently at a problem can distort rather than enlighten, while relaxing one's focus actually enhances one's ability to see. For nearly two years, Abe Kulp had been tightly focused on the search for an idealized director, without success. Once Kulp stopped looking for an individual, he found just the individual he was looking for.

*   *   *

Early in 1961, C. Stewart Sheppard, dean of the Graduate School of Business and Public Administration at Cornell, realized that he had grown "weary of juggling a faculty of diverse interests" and decided to resign. A native Welshman, Sheppard had served in the U. S. Army during World War II as a naturalized citizen and had been educated in economics and business at New York University and Columbia. Sheppard had been on the N.Y.U. faculty from 1948 to 1956 as a professor of economics, while concurrently acting as executive director of the Joint Committee on Education of the American Securities Industry (ASI). As such, he was essentially a liaison between the financial community's academics and practitioners, for his function was to bring "ten professors each year to study the inner workings of Wall Street . . . [so as] to educate the educators regarding financial realities."

Sheppard had spent the five years following his association with NYU and the ASI as dean at Cornell. When his friend, Charles C. Abbott, dean at the newly-established Graduate School of Business at the University of Virginia, suggested that he join with him in "developing the first school of its kind in the South," Sheppard found the offer "compellingly attractive." Abbott himself was a recent addition to Virginia, having accepted the deanship in 1954, after 16 years as professor of banking and finance at Harvard. Under the presidency of Edgar F. Shannon, the University of Virginia was in the process of shedding its bourbon-and-hounds image and transforming itself into a first-rate university, and Abbott's task was to establish a highly regarded MBA case method program. In 1961, he invited his friend Stewart Sheppard to become a professor of Business Administration and return to teaching. By April of that year Sheppard's acceptance had been approved, effective in September.

Two months before Sheppard agreed to go to Virginia and resume teaching, Abe Kulp had begun writing business school deans about the "newly established Institute of Chartered Financial Analysts" and its need for an administration. "We have an open mind at this time, as to whether an arrangement should be made with the selected individual or a university," said Kulp. The location of the Institute would be determined later—but would likely be at the selected university. Among those contacted was Dean Floyd Bond of Michigan. David Williams, the Institute's vice president, had written to Abe Kulp the previous December to inform him that Detroit Society member Jim Waterman had hinted there was "some possibility of interest" among the business faculty at Ann Arbor. Gil Palmer expressed a similar idea: "I keep thinking of the University of Michigan, not because I am an alumnus, but because it seems to fit the bill with respect to location, status, and my guess that they would be particularly eager to do the job."

In fact they were. Professor Waterman of David Williams' acquaintance, who was acting as dean of Business Administration, responded with Michigan's active "interest and cooperation" and embarassedly offered himself as potential director. At 58, Waterman was older than Kulp's ideal, but had 34 years of educational experience and recently had helped set up the finance program for a new graduate business school in France. Waterman's name had actually come up some time earlier but he had not yet been contacted, perhaps because he had been on leave during the 1959-60 academic year.

Around the same time Waterman and Michigan came under consideration, Federation and Institute treasurer George Hansen mentioned to Abe Kulp that the University of Virginia might be a place for the Institute. Virginia's dean, Charles Abbott, was a director of Keystone Custodian Funds where Hansen managed a research department. Hansen knew and respected Abbott and suggested that he be contacted. Kulp made a note to himself to do so, added Virginia to the growing list of schools to write to, and on February 27 sent Charles Abbott a letter describing the Institute and its need for both a director and a physical location. Like Michigan, Virginia was willing.

Abbott wrote back on March 3 stressing his own and President Shannon's interest and indicating that he had "a couple of ideas about possible people. . . . " After a phone conversation with Kulp on March 13, Abbott sent a formal description of his fledgling graduate school and arranged to meet with Kulp in Washington on Saturday, March 18. The outcome of this meeting was that Abbott was to submit a formal proposal for the directorship and to meet with Federation members in April. As luck would have it, the incoming Federation president was George Stevenson Kemp of Richmond, and the Federation's annual meeting was to be held in his home city, 75 miles from Charlottesville, the location of the University of Virginia.

On April 17, 1961, Abe Kulp, George Hansen, and Federation president Jeremy Jenks visited the University of Virginia. At that time Charlottesville was just a small southern town in the foothills of the Blue Ridge Mountains. The Dogwood Festival held each year in the typically warm weather of mid-April was in full swing. This year, however, the festivities were accompanied by temperatures in the low 50s and a threat of scattered frost. Apparently, the inhospitable weather did not have a negative effect on their impression of the University for the three men liked what they saw in Virginia.

One person they did not get to see on the visit, of course, was Stewart Sheppard. Sheppard's name had been submitted for the directorship just four days before. While Sheppard had eagerly agreed to come to Virginia the following fall and resume teaching, it must have taken substantial persuasion on Abbott's part to convince his old Wall Street friend, who admittedly "was in retreat from administrative responsibilities," to consider spending half of his anticipated academic leisure on administering the new Institute. The arrangement, Sheppard jokingly lamented later, was to leave him "half free and half slave."

Prior to the Charlottesville trip, Kulp, Hansen and Jenks had gone to the University of Michigan to meet with Jim Waterman. Waterman impressed Kulp as "one of the finest men you could ever meet," and Michigan was well equiped to handle an Institute. In addition to Waterman's services, Michigan could offer an established business program at a prominent university and a staff that included Douglas Hayes—long of interest to those searching for a director. Several of the Michigan faculty, moreover, were active Federation members. Yet, however pleased Kulp was with Michigan, he continued to consider Virginia. After two years of having individuals and institutions prove either unsuitable or unavailable, it must have been gratifying to have two superior schools actively pursuing the Institute.

Kulp, Jenks and Hansen returned to New York from Charlottesville on April 20 and immediately met with Stewart Sheppard. No one recorded the details of that meeting, but it must have been one of mutual satisfaction, for Sheppard ended up expressing "evident interest" in the objectives of the Institute and Kulp ended up writing him later that very day requesting a detailed vita, "so that [he could] submit a comprehensive report of [Sheppard's] background with [his] recommendation to the Executive Council of [the] Institute on Sunday, April 30, at [the] annual meeting in Richmond." Sheppard's name had been submitted only ten days earlier, but by the end of the month he was the Institute's long-awaited director.

Even as Kulp was hinting broadly to Sheppard the likelihood of his being chosen as director, he was writing to the Institute's councilors and officers indicating that of the two schools under serious consideration, "the balance is distinctly in favor of Virginia." What struck the balance in Virginia's favor? In his memoirs of his affiliation with the Institute, Stewart Sheppard maintains that Kulp's committee "backed into its decision to affiliate the embryo Institute of Chartered Financial Analysts with the University of Virginia" by knowing what they didn't want. To some extent this is true. The officers did not want to locate the ICFA in an urban center where it would be subject to pressure from the financial community; neither did they want to be at a university "so complex that it would overlook the adequate nurture" a new program needed. But Sheppard modestly disregards the obvious positive attractions of Virginia: himself, Charles Abbott, and the University's desire to increase its prestige. As Gilbert Palmer—himself a proponent of Michigan—recalled, although Michigan's reputation in the early 1960s was greater than Virginia's, the problem with Michigan was that the ICFA wanted to be an "important part of the institution it joined"; they couldn't be guaranteed that at Ann Arbor. At Virginia's energetically evolving graduate business school, however, a position of central importance was assured. Virginia had more to offer in "the unusual combination of Dean Abbott and Dean Sheppard," as Abe Kulp put it, and it also had more to gain.

CHAPTER THREE
The First Examinations

The men who founded and organized the Institute of Chartered Financial Analysts got just about everything right: they got the right proposal, they located the right university, and they chose in Stewart Sheppard an energetic director who would help the Institute grow to over three thousand members in his 11 year tenure. But one thing they consistently got wrong was the amount of time required to get the Institute going. When Abe Kulp submitted his first detailed report to the Federation in 1955, he bravely predicted that "a complete setup would be in operation by the fall of 1956." Six years later, when he had finally found Dr. Sheppard, he announced in the *Financial Analysts Journal* that the new director's time would be devoted to "devising appropriate examinations which we hope to hold in the fall of 1962." But in mid-January of that year, six months before the examinations needed to be ready, Kulp and Sheppard found themselves riding back from a "sobering" day-long consultation with the American College of Life Underwriters at Bryn Mawr, feeling "very subdued" and agreeing that the ICFA was not at all ready to mount an examination and grading session such as they had just witnessed. Sheppard remembers it as a humbling moment: "Here we were, we had everything announced, and we weren't ready."

The Institute was unprepared to meet its mission, but not because its officers and director had been idle. Even before his official appointment on September 1, 1961, Stewart Sheppard had begun the task of organizing, by working with the Executive Council on forming Articles of Incorporation and By-laws, formalized on January 30, 1962, and setting objectives for the first examinations. Sheppard faced various housekeeping tasks as well: he had to work out the mechanics of accepting and processing applications in conjunction with local Societies, of setting fee schedules and exam dates and finding exam centers. Although Sheppard felt fortunate in being able "to start from scratch and avoid hindrances from vested interests," he did in fact have to reinvent the wheel a few times in those first months.

But beyond the everyday problems that beset any new organization, a larger philosophical question posed by Stewart Sheppard needed to be addressed: "What should be the hallmark of this profession?" The CFA should not, he argued, "be a self-conferred cachet signifying financial acumen." Instead, the Institute's charter should rest on a solid foundation:

> a common body of knowledge to be acquired only through systematic study; rigorous objective examinations conceived and conducted by the Institute with headquarters sufficiently isolated and insulated from industry involvements; and a code of professional ethics that would insure a commonality of integrity among CFA charter holders.

The Federation leaders who pushed for analyst accreditation had recognized the need for such a firm foundation years before. Abe Kulp, even while immersed in the politics of getting an institute approved, wrote a note to himself in 1957 that the proposed program must be "adamant on high standards," with examinations both "comprehensive" and set at a "high level."

Such excellence could not be the product of haste, as Kulp and Sheppard knew only too well. "Our program is charged with such great importance," Sheppard wrote to publisher Richard D. Irwin, who also had attended the CLU session in Bryn Mawr in January 1962, "that we ought not to be stampeded in any way into taking any premature action on the examinations. . . . When this program starts, it must be the most efficient of its kind, and we cannot afford to have any bottlenecks in the pipeline." Thus, though Sheppard and Kulp left their day of observing the Life Underwriters examination and grading sessions with "a deep feeling of humility," they were "not discouraged in the slightest." Rather, they were, as Kulp had earlier phrased it, still "adamant on high standards" and willing to face the consequences of pushing the date for the first examination back to June 1963, in order to set before the experienced analysts who would take it an exam that would in no sense be a giveaway, and whose rigor would establish the "values and integrity" of the Institute itself and uphold those of the university under whose aegis it was to be given.

The debate on examination format and content had begun effectively at a June 19, 1961, Executive Council meeting. There, Sheppard and Charles Abbott discussed in detail with the Institute's officers the "educational problems involved" in setting up an examination program. To get a sense of what was needed, the council decided that Sheppard should formulate sample questions and exams—with the guidance of "other academic people" from outside the Virginia faculty—and submit them to the council for final approval. The council also discussed at length Solomon's original exam format and came up with a substantial revision: exams I and II were to be combined into a single eight-hour test; exam III would likewise be eight hours. But the intermediate exam was, as Stewart Sheppard recalled, subject to considerable debate: "our options were to require a thesis or to require technical analysis [to] bridge the testing of fundamentals in examination one and sophisticated management experience in the third examination." At the June 19 meeting the council voted in favor of requiring a thesis of "independent and original research in an area related to . . . professional financial interest."

The thesis requirement turned out to be short-lived. Throughout the summer and fall of 1961, Stewart Sheppard had been preparing a descriptive brochure of the Institute for submission to Richard D. Irwin, who had agreed to act as the Institute's publisher. Before going to Irwin's design staff, the draft brochure was circulated to the Institute's council and officers. Abe Kulp, who had been consulting with the American Institute for Property and Life Underwriters, Inc. and the American College of Life Underwriters (both in nearby Bryn Mawr), sent the draft brochure to Harry J. Loman, the A.I.P.L.U. president. Loman responded with detailed notes on December 7, 1961. Both Kulp and Federation president Steve Kemp sent copies of his letter to Stewart Sheppard, so germane were Loman's remarks. One aspect of the proposed Institute program to which Loman took particular exception was the thesis requirement:

> You will probably find the administration of the thesis requirement a terrible headache. Such a thing is difficult enough when a candidate is preparing a thesis under the close supervision of a faculty member. To administer this type of program on a national scale, so that all persons will be treated in an equal manner will be most difficult.

Loman's points proved to be well taken. The matter of the thesis requirement was again taken up at the February 26, 1962, Executive Council Meeting. It turned out that support for the thesis was lukewarm at best. Stewart Sheppard had found the thesis proposal "somewhat" attractive in that it might be of use "in developing a research base for the examination program," but had recognized that it would be "difficult to monitor independent research effort." Charles Abbott too had had some doubts. While he had originally liked the idea, he had come to see its impracticality. The council minutes note that subsequent discussion "produced no support for the thesis requirement and indicated that there had been considerable reservation as to its desirability on the part of all those present." As a result, the thesis requirement was dropped and the examination structure revised. Examination 1 was to cover financial accounting, institutions, and security analysis; Examination 2, economic growth and fluctuations, and "national and international problems," particularly emphasizing applied security analysis; Examination 3, investment timing and portfolio balance, selection of industries and securities, and conflict of interest questions to test "the analyst's personal ethics." With the notable new inclusion of a question on ethics, this exam format was greatly similar to Ezra Solomon's original structure as revised by Abe Kulp in April 1960.

*   *   *

It was one thing to formulate examination content but quite a different matter to formulate challenging questions. "Developing the initial examination," Stewart Sheppard remarked, was a "relatively lonely experience." Sheppard's closest associates, the Institute's officers, "were obviously ineligible to participate in the forming of their own examination"—particularly one testing conflicts of interest. Sheppard's allies in working up the early examinations, then, were to be the "other academic people" from outside Virginia suggested by the Executive Council in June 1961. Such outstanding academics had been found quickly. By September 1961 Marshall Ketchum of the University of Chicago and Douglas Hayes of Michigan joined Charles Abbott on what would soon be called the Council of examiners. Hayes and Ketchum were both old friends of Sheppard from his Wall Street days. Ketchum was, in Abe Kulp's opinion, a particularly valuable addition to the Institute because "his interest and cooperation [would] help a lot in a large part of the country." By June 1962 Eric Kierans, president of the Montreal Stock Exchange and lecturer at McGill had been added as the Canadian advisor, while Corliss Anderson, a recently retired partner in the consulting firm Duff, Anderson and Clark, was taken on as the industry representative. A member of the finance faculty at Northwestern, Anderson had outstanding academic credentials as well. To insure their own impartiality, the examiners agreed to waive their eligibility for the upcoming examinations.

The visit by Kulp and Sheppard to the CLU sessions in Bryn Mawr resulted not only in a postponement of the first exams from the fall of 1962 to the spring of 1963, but also in a reassessment of how many high quality tests they could compose. Like Kulp, Sheppard wanted to be sure the Institute's exams were suitably challenging. The difficulties of preparing three comprehensive exams were such that the Executive Council voted on February 26, 1962, to administer only Examination 3 the following year—the "grandfather" exam for which they were all eligible. Stewart Sheppard's brochure was to be available by April 1962; the study materials and outlines by September. Candidate applications were due in January 1963. It was under this framework that the Council of Examiners began to compose the first exam.

In the fall of 1961, C. Ray Smith, recently graduated from Virginia's MBA program, had agreed to return to the University—"just for one year"—and teach accounting in the graduate business program. Smith was given the office next to Stewart Sheppard's on the mezzanine in Monroe Hall. The Institute's new director found in his neighbor an able friend and ally for the "lonely" task of constructing the first CFA exam, and on February 26, 1962, asked the Institute's officers to appoint Smith as his assistant, "working one-half time during the academic year and full time during the summer." When Smith assumed the post on June 1, 1962, his plans to spend "one year" at Virginia were scuttled forever: for the next nine years he aided Sheppard in the large and small business of the Institute, and even now—some 25 years later—continues to teach at Virginia's Darden School.

Sheppard, Smith and the Council of Examiners had an exceedingly important task before them in the preparation of the first examination. It was, in Stewart Sheppard's mind, the "one mile-stone on the path to the C.F.A. program" most predictive of the success or failure of the Institute. After years of struggling with the "grandfather" issue, the Institute's officers and administrators knew that this first test, which would be given only to "regular members of a constituent society of the Financial Analysts Federation prior to December 31, 1956 . . . who were born on or before December 31, 1918," had to be pitched at the right level. It was desirable, of course, that the leading analysts in the country, who would make up most of the initial candidates, become members of the Institute. The exam thus could not be arbitrarily or capriciously difficult. But the Institute could not sacrifice its reputation just to get notable analysts among its members. The ICFA, which intended to be the bellwether of integrity and high standards for the industry, must establish its credibility by giving a rigorous examination. This test was itself a test—for the Institute. Its successful passage would carry great symbolic weight.

The work of preparing the exam began in earnest in the spring of 1962, with Charles Abbott and the other examiners submitting questions to Stewart Sheppard. By late summer, sample examinations and alternative questions had been circulated among the Institute's Board of Trustees (known as the Executive Council prior to incorporation on January 30, 1962). At the September 10 Board meeting there was extended debate among those practitioners and their academic Council of Examiners on the appropriate content of the exam and how each question should be weighed in the grading. There was also controversy over whether or not the trustees should take a trial examination—not to test themselves, but to test the exam. Dr. Sheppard had proposed abolishing this "dry run," fearing "criticism to the effect that the Board of Trustees might have some special advantage" when they later took the actual exam the following June. The trustees, confident of their own integrity, did not feel such criticism was warranted "as long as the questions as contained on the final examinations were not known by the trustees and if all candidates for the examination received sample questions. . . . " The advantages of establishing grading standards through the use of such a trial examination outweighed any anticipated criticism. As a result, the Board unanimously agreed that Stewart Sheppard administer the trial exam, "subject to the understanding that the grading not be reported back" to anyone answering the questions.

Four days after the Board meeting, Sheppard sent each member a sample series of questions, accompanied by a questionnaire to be filled out after taking the test under simulated exam conditions, i.e., writing in long-hand and giving no more than one-half hour to each of the eight questions. Sheppard weighed the trustees' responses and decided that considerably more work was in order. Consequently, he, Ray Smith, and the Examiners sat down and constructed a "dummy" exam. Feeling that both the examining and grading processes needed further refinement, Sheppard had this "dummy" exam given to a group of Canadian analysts in the fall of 1962, administered and graded as if it were the actual test. The Canadians were chosen because they were a fairly homogeneous group, and being geographically removed could ensure the confidentiality of this trial examination. Stewart Sheppard was determined that no one connected with the Institute would have—or even appear to have—an "insider's" advantage in taking the real exam the following spring.

The Canadians filled out questionnaires about the appropriateness and adequacy of the test. Their comments ranged from "excellent" to "sorry to come out with such a negative attitude but that is exactly my reaction." Because Exam III dealt with the decision-making abilities of senior analysts, Sheppard opted for more of a case-method approach, and revised the "dummy exam" accordingly. This revision became the basis for the "Examination III—Sample," which was available to all candidates as part of the Study Guide in February 1963. One month later, the "Preliminary Draft" of the actual June examination was sent to the five-member Council of Examiners in the strictest confidence, emblazoned with a warning that the questions were "Not To Be Discussed With Anyone Not On The Council." Some dates, company names, and financial data would be changed to make the June printing current, but in March 1963 the Institute reached a milestone: it was ready to give its first examination.

By March, the Institute had received 318 registrations and expected to have approximately 300 candidates actually sit for the exam—a remarkable show of interest from the established analysts. To help them review, the Institute's administration had prepared a study guide which it made available to all candidates. The project had been started by Pierce Lumpkin, Sheppard's temporary assistant when he became director, and was completed by Ray Smith. The guides were ready in mid-December 1962 and contained all the articles on the reading list as well as "sample questions in all areas."

Throughout 1962, Eugene M. Lerner, a faculty member at C.U.N.Y.'s Baruch College, had been preparing a book of readings for candidates. A forerunner of the *CFA Readings in Financial Analysis*, Lerner's book was to be a compilation of relevant articles from *The Financial Analysts Journal,* arranged by topic and keyed to the body of knowledge upon which exam questions would be based. Lerner also wrote a student manual of synopses and guidelines. Because Lerner's book—which had official approval from the Institute—was not to be published until March 1963, Stewart Sheppard obtained permission from Richard D. Irwin, the Institute's and Lerner's publisher, to print the relevant articles on "Portfolio Analysis and Management" in the Institute's study guides. Through this one-time arrangement, those who wished to prepare in advance were able to do so. At the same time, study groups were formed. Trustee Grant Torrance of Kansas City had brought up the idea of study group formation as early as September 1961. These groups had been encouraged by the Institute, and in the spring of 1963 many of the country's leading analysts sat down with their peers and reviewed.

The candidates faced an interesting challenge. They had to review the subject matter of their profession, but more importantly, they had to accustom themselves to the idea of taking an exam. The youngest candidates were in their middle 40s and had been out of school for 15 or 20 years. Thirty-three of the candidates were over 60. Forty years in the profession would be of tremendous benefit in mastering the subject matter of the exam, but 40 years out of college weakened one's test-taking skills. Moreover, the analysts who sat for the first exam had reached sufficient status in their organizations and were accustomed to dictating, not writing. The sheer physical strain of sitting in a chair and writing for five hours was in itself worrisome to many of the older analysts.

Ragnar Naess of the New York Society recalled that people in his study group were "very nervous," and felt "there was really something at stake"—so much so, in fact, that many Society members were reluctant to take the exam. George Hansen recalled that those in the Boston study group took the preparation "very, very seriously." There was a healthy competition among firms in Boston to see who would be most successful on the exam. Hansen and E. Linwood Savage "closeted" themselves the weekend before the test and "asked questions back and forth." This may not have been the most judicious way to study, in Hansen's opinion, but "it helped a great deal."

Hartman Butler of the Chicago Society had a different experience. In his words: "Nothing that I studied helped me on the exam, but the *fact* that I had studied gave me a degree of confidence which enabled me to pass." Both Butler's firm, Duff and Phelps, and the Chicago Society had actively encouraged analyst participation in the CFA program and sponsored formal study groups. In St. Louis, where only three analysts had registered, Carl Beckers studied alone. Recalling his determination to pass, Beckers remarked, "I studied harder for that than for any exam in my life." In Cleveland, former Federation president Gil Palmer sat down with 12 or so other analysts, talking over what to study and reviewing exam-taking techniques. "We took this very seriously," Palmer recalled, "It was no joke: we were very much interested in passing it." Like Carl Beckers, those senior analysts in Cleveland, and throughout this country and Canada, felt "proud and determined to pass."

The exam's administration on June 15, 1963, came at a most propitious time for those with such pride in themselves and their profession. Since 1961, the Securities and Exchange Commission had been investigating the industry. Spurred by what the Commission called the "hyperactive new issue market" of 1961, the SEC continued its investigation through 1962, casting a particularly jaundiced eye on the wild trading in the spring of that year which culminated in the Memorial Day weekend "market break." The commissioners were particularly concerned with the roles of investment counselors and analysts, upon whose research investment advice was based. They did not like what they saw. "As to the performance of the function of research and analysis as such," the Commission reported, "there are no entry controls at all." Citing the ludicrous example of a 19-year-old boy who published a market letter called "The Trading Floor" and whose research was based on the opinions of two cousins, ages 14 and 20, who were "fanatically interested in the stock market," the Commission wondered who was protecting the interests of the public with regard to investment risk.

By the time the first part of the SEC's *Special Study of Securities Markets* was issued in April 1963, the ICFA had come into being and was preparing to give its first exam. The study acknowledged the Institute's aim of "achieving professional recognition," but feared it would lack sufficient strength. Unless the ICFA forcefully barred "unqualified persons from engaging in analytic activities without supervision," it concluded, "the program would seem to point to only limited benefits for the public." The Commission's criticism was misplaced. Though the Institute would take great care in succeeding years to safeguard the ethics of its members, it was never designed to act as a police force for the entire industry, as Stewart Sheppard informed *The Wall Street Journal* in May 1963:

> We want to get at the policy makers . . . men who are conscious of the professional nature of financial analysis. We hope they'll recognize the importance of the CFA designation and pursue it voluntarily.

The Institute's charter—which could be rescinded at any time for behavior duly judged unethical—was to be the exclusive possession of those who met the Institute's standards of knowledge and conduct. But it was not the Institute's purpose to exclude from the financial community persons "unqualified" to do research. The Institute's charter was, in Sheppard's words, "a public warranty"; that those who held it had demonstrated to the Institute their knowledge, their decision-making ability, and their continuing high ethical standards.

The Commission misconstrued the Institute's purpose; it also failed to understand the Institute's real importance. As Abe Kulp told the same *Journal* reporter, the SEC study "greatly underestimates the significance of this movement." Kulp was well aware that work toward analyst accreditation long predated the SEC's recent stirrings. The movement had evolved within the Federation's leadership, which had willingly taken the time needed to generate a challenging and worthwhile program. However, the SEC's skepticism would have to be met: successful implementation of the CFA program would be of great benefit in keeping analyst regulation in the hands of the analysts themselves. The 278 men and six women who sat for the first CFA examination on June 15, 1963, therefore, had a good deal at stake. In addition to their personal pride, these experienced analysts bore with them the future of the analyst community itself.

Two weeks later the professional grading staff — which included Pierce Lumpkin, William Rotch, and C. F. Sargent — began the serious task of evaluating the tests. When grading was completed in late July, Smith and Sheppard reviewed each exam. Two hundred and sixty-eight of the candidates had passed and 16 failed. The high passing rate reflected the expertise of those who took the examination. The majority of those who failed graciously acknowledged their lack of preparation and made plans to take the test again. One unsuccessful candidate, however, a "partner in charge of the research department of a major Wall Street firm," suggested irately to Virginia's president, Edgar Shannon, that Stewart Sheppard be dismissed from the faculty.

*   *   *

On September 14, 1963, the Board of Trustees — all of whom had taken and passed the new exam — met in Charlottesville. The minutes of their meeting begin routinely enough with a treasurer's report from George Hansen, a question from Dutton Morehouse about unclear wording on the new pamphlet, and a report from Stewart Sheppard on the June 1963 exams. This last item was of great significance to these men who had labored so long to make the CFA a reality. The next paragraph, however, recorded a truly momentous event. William C. Norby, president of the Financial Analysts Federation, requested the floor and cited Article II, Section I of the Institute's Bylaws, which read:

> The initiating members, as defined in the Articles of Incorporation, shall serve until the occurrence of the earlier of the following events: (i) the receipt of 200 persons of professional designation as chartered financial analysts, or (ii) the expiration of 10 years from the date hereof. Upon the occurrence of either of such events, as determined in

accordance with the by-laws, the membership of all initiating members shall cease and expire.

Acting in his capacity as Federation president, Norby dissolved the Initiating Group. From that day on, the Institute would have only chartered members.

On its first administration, the CFA examination had generated so much interest and produced so many successful candidates that a predicted decade-long goal had been surpassed in one sitting. The Board members, forward-thinking leaders of their profession, had reason to be proud. One, however, might have been slightly chagrined. Treasurer George Hansen, who holds the Institute Charter Number One, had a year before been reluctant to let Stewart Sheppard purchase a "four-drawer file cabinet, not even new." Sheppard had convinced him to approve the purchase, with the understanding that it should be sufficient for about 10 years. One year later, after the administration of a single exam, Sheppard's 10 year file cabinet already needed replacing.

CHAPTER FOUR
Growing Pains

In August 1963, shortly before the first CFA charters were awarded, Stewart Sheppard sent University of Virginia president Edgar F. Shannon a progress report on the first year of the Institute. Citing the enthusiasm, creativity and dedication of the Institute staff and the "many statesmanlike financiers throughout the U.S. and Canada who, since 1945, have dreamed of the day when professionalism would supplant opportunism in the financial markets of the world," Sheppard detailed his and Charles Abbott's "justifiable pride" in the Institute's stature. But Sheppard also wondered whether his friend and mentor Abbott might not have mixed feelings about their great success:

> On the one hand, he must feel an inordinate pride in the successful launching of an enterprise that lends worthy luster to a school that is still of tender years. But, on the other hand, he must at times experience a degree of apprehension that this lusty infant will insist on ever-increasing spatial requirements as a natural concomitant of the maturation years.

In fact, this "lusty infant" was outdoing its analogue. In 1964, the Institute grew sixfold—to 1,742 candidates from 284 candidates in

1963. The University of Virginia was indeed pressed to find sufficient room for the staff.

In addition to straining the capacity of Virginia's business school, the ICFA had begun to test its relationship with the Financial Analysts Federation. William C. Norby, who in his capacity as Federation president had dissolved the Institute's Initiating Group and established its charter members, became aware "early on of a political problem between the FAF and the ICFA." The crux of the problem lay in the very nature of the two organizations: an independent organization of individual professionals would necessarily have different goals and methods than—in Norby's words—"a federation of societies which retained considerable independence [from each other] and indulged in all too frequent political infighting." Beyond these inevitable differences, the Federation already had begun to view the Institute with a bit of suspicion, fearing a competitive rather than a cooperative relationship.

In reality, the relationship between the organizations was more often close than strained. The Institute was financially and spiritually indebted to the Federation for its existence, and its officers were well aware of this debt. Moreover, Federation president William Norby had been actively promoting the acceptance of the CFA as the standard for the investment community. In January 1964, Norby had begun writing to various regulatory bodies—NASD, NYSE and MSE among them—about adopting the CFA as a qualification for research personnel. The SEC's *Special Study of Securities Markets* had emphasized the need for some formal qualification of such persons, and Norby suggested attainment of the CFA as an adequate and necessary credential. Addressing the Federation's directors in April 1964, Norby detailed his position on the CFA versus possible alternative designations of professional competence for analysts:

> Our viewpoint in the FAF has been that if analysts are to be qualified by one of the self-regulatory agencies, the CFA designation should be the criterion and not some other standard or examination for financial analysts developed by

that particular self-regulatory agency. The uniformity of one designation for any financial analyst would eliminate confusion with the public and enhance the value of the CFA charter, as well as facilitate mobility of analysts within the several segments of the investment industry. Furthermore, we think it would be most difficult for anyone to duplicate what our Institute has already accomplished.

Norby's staunch promotion of the CFA charter did not go unheeded. In June 1964, the New York Stock Exchange adopted Rule 344, which specified that supervisory research personnel might offer the possession of an Institute charter as one of three sufficient qualifications.

The successful launching of the CFA exam program had sparked interest beyond the analyst community. By the fall of 1963, according to Stewart Sheppard, the Institute was "being courted by such matrimonial prospects as the Investment Counsel Association of America, the Investment Bankers Association of America and . . . the New York Institute of Finance." Norby and the Federation often acted as liaison. In subsequent years, the Institute would administer a Chartered Investment Counselor program for the ICAA and act as consultant in many other cases. Some proposals were more acceptable than others, however. Stewart Sheppard recalled the astonishment which appeared on the faces of the Institute's board when he read them one invitation he'd received—from the warden of Sing Sing state penitentiary: "It appeared that a number of the inmates were of previous importance in Wall Street and the warden felt that their candidacy in the C.F.A. program would be a healthy rehabilitative measure." It was a rare occurrence, Sheppard noted, to see the Board of Trustees so completely nonplussed.

*   *   *

The rehabilitation of Wall Streeters gone astray was hardly the Institute's mission, but perhaps what the warden at Sing Sing had in mind was educating the inmates in more ethical conduct. Ethics were the Institute's purview and continuing focus. The FAF had formally adopted a Code of Ethics in 1962. David G.

Watterson, who assumed chairmanship of the Federation's Professional Ethics and Standards Committee when Abe Kulp became ICFA president, had assembled a committee of distinguished analysts to write the code. Particularly helpful, in Watterson's opinion, were Michigan's Douglas Hayes, one of the Institute's first examiners, and Leonard Barlow of Toronto, later an ICFA president. The Federation's code, which Watterson prepared "without benefit of legal counsel," spelled out the member analysts' responsibilities to the public; to customers, clients, and employers; and to corporate management and others furnishing information. This Code of Ethics was adopted by all but three member societies throughout the next year—the three being New York, Boston and Washington, which had their own codes. By the spring of 1964, a set of guidelines and interpretations authored by Watterson's committee had been added to the code.

At the same time, Watterson was heading an Ethical Standards Committee for the Institute, whose purpose was to formulate a Code of Ethics appropriate for charterholders. It was particularly incumbent upon the Institute to adopt such a code quickly, because ethics questions were to appear on all three of the 1964 exams. In fact, the conflict of interest problem which appeared at the end of the Institute's premiere exam in 1963 had proven to be somewhat difficult for the first candidates, much to the surprise of Stewart Sheppard and the trustees. Sheppard recalls, "It was felt by many, including myself, that [the ethics problems] would be give-away questions but would be justified if they demonstrated the importance of proper moral conduct to a C.F.A. holder." It turned out, however, that the ethics questions challenged the candidates, "who either failed to detect the ethical problem or were unable to provide alternative solutions." Concerned that by placing the ethical problems at the end of the exams they might be giving such vital material short shrift—since the candidates would be fatigued when they got to them—Charles Abbott and the examiners suggested to Sheppard and the trustees that the sequence of questions be rotated. This practice was put into effect with the 1965 examinations.

In September 1963, Stewart Sheppard drafted a CFA Code of Ethics, drawing heavily on the FAF's newly adopted code, but changing the wording in several places to refer to Chartered Financial Analysts. This draft was submitted to Abe Kulp and David Watterson, who made minor revisions. The new version was circulated among the Institute's Ethical Standards Committee in January 1964. The consensus of that group was not to rewrite the Federation's code, which, as Sheppard had noted earlier, was so well worded that it was "difficult to improve upon it." They chose instead to adopt it "almost verbatim," in Watterson's words, "together with a set of 'Guidelines' to cover more specifically the problem areas which appear to need particular attention as well as the necessary references to use of the C.F.A. designation." Watterson's committee members, along with William Norby, Douglas Hayes, and Stewart Sheppard, all contributed to the drafting of the guidelines. Both the code and the guidelines were submitted at the March 14, 1964, Institute Board meetings, and were unanimously adopted.

These initial guidelines (which are printed as Appendix A) closely paralleled those adopted by the Federation and detailed the CFA's desired behavior in regard to the public, clients, associates, and employers in obeying "both the letter and spirit of the law" governing financial matters. Likewise, the guidelines indicated the CFA's responsibilities regarding borrowed material, independent practice, payment of fees, and personal financial transactions. The Institute added one guideline on the proper use and display of the CFA designation and—most significant—a published declaration that violations of code or guidelines would be "regarded as cause for termination by appropriate action of the Board of Trustees . . . [of the] right to use the C.F.A. designation."

Although the Institute was many years away from establishing a rigorous ethics enforcement procedure, the Trustees had assumed from the outset a seriousness of purpose regarding ethical as well as educational standards. Unique among comparable professional groups at the time, the Institute wrote into its ethical "Guidelines," candidate brochures, and Bylaws the proviso that the CFA charter could—and would—be revoked if it was determined that the holder had violated the Institute's professional ethical standards. Furthermore, as Stewart Sheppard noted, any man or woman entering the CFA program had to agree to this in order to become a candidate: "The C.F.A. candidate, upon initial registration in the program, signed an official statement to the effect that in the event of a violation of the code, either in the examinations process or after receiving the charter, the C.F.A. designation may be revoked." After 1968, moreover, charterholders were required to fill out an annual questionnaire on their ethical conduct.

The first instance of a case involving ethical standards began with what in retrospect appears to be a minor infraction. On June 2, 1964, the First National Bank of Boston and Old Colony Trust Company ran an ad in the *Boston Globe* which showed an elderly lady asking "You mean that's all I have to do—buy low and sell high?" The ad's copy went to "explain" why this particular bank and trust, where there were men "whose life work is analyzing opportunities in every worthwhile field of investment," was the best place for her money. In the judgment of some, this ad was in dubious taste and might even be the "flamboyant advertising" specifically interdicted by the Institute's Code of Ethics. Although chartered analysts were not mentioned in the ad, at least one Institute member was a senior officer there, so the Trustees passed the matter on to David Watterson's Ethical Standards Committee for review. The committee members' responses to the ad varied from "flamboyant and extravagant" to "thought it a pretty good ad." However, the consensus was that although the ad might be objectionable to some, responsibility for it lay with the institution, not the individual; the disciplining of organizations was beyond the Institute's province. Thus, they reported at the Board of Trustees meeting on September 12, 1964, that no action was recommended in the case. They further stated that "the committee should concern itself primarily with the conduct of CFAs as individuals, rather than with the organizations and institutions with which the CFA might be affiliated, except in instances where the CFA might be directly responsible for the policies of the organization." At the same board meeting, it was determined that while the Ethical Standards Committee would review all complaints that it received of possible violations, "disciplinary action would be taken only by the Board of Trustees." It would be several years before such action was taken against an Institute member. The Board of Trustees and the Ethics Committee had nevertheless begun, with this early case, to define their respective tasks.

* * *

The September 1964 board meeting also saw a refinement of roles for the Institute's various committees. A year earlier, the board had established an Admissions Committee, an Ethical Standards Committee, an Exam Review Committee, a Public and Industry Relations Committee, and a Research and Publications Committee, in addition to the already extant Council of Examiners, which as of 1964 was made up only of CFAs. Except for Exam Review, which was composed entirely of Trustees, the committees were formed to involve members in the ongoing business of running the Institute, and to take some of the burden off of the administrators in Charlottesville, who were reeling from the program's rapid expansion.

The Admissions Committee was charged with resolving questions about candidates' eligibility and reviewing applications for reexamination. The Ethical Standards Committee concerned itself with both violations of the Institute's code and with abuses of the CFA designation. The duty of the Public and Industry Relations Committee was to further develop relationships with the SEC, ICAA, NASD, and so forth, which had been initiated by Federation president William Norby. These committees paralleled—and occasionally joined with—similar Federation committees. However, given the Institute's unique function as the educational and testing arm of the analyst community, the Council of Examiners and the Research and Publications Committee had no FAF counterparts.

The Council of Examiners' role as composer of the examinations would be complemented by the work of the Research and Publications Committee, which was to read manuscripts submitted for publication under the Institute's imprint, and to find new articles suitable for inclusion in the annually revised study guides, continuously reviewing those retained in subsequent editions. In addition, the Research and Publications Committee would encourage the publication of research articles and monographs on topics not adequately covered by existing materials available to analysts. Thus they would establish the parameters of subjects on which an analyst could be tested, while the Council of Examiners would complete the circle by constructing the actual exam. In succeeding years, the Research and Publications Committee would, in a sense, come to define the profession of financial analysis by determining what constituted the fields of knowledge necessary for professional analytical endeavor.

Forming, expanding, and refining the various Institute committees between the fall of 1963 and the winter of 1964 was a milestone for the ICFA, for it firmly established the principle of voluntarism that guides the Institute to this day. While a salaried professional staff was essential to the daily business of the Institute, the ICFA's early leaders determined that major policy decisions would be placed in the hands of those chartered members voluntarily committed to the betterment of the Institute and the profession. In 1964, his last year as Institute president, Abe Kulp organized the committees, carefully balancing "experience, stature, geographic location and type of employer" in choosing committee members. He wanted the Institute to utilize the diversity of its population and thus draw in as much industry-wide support as possible. The committees also functioned as a seedbed for future Institute leaders—committee volunteers whose work in forming Institute policies regarding admissions, ethics, research, industry relations, and examinations prepared them for later, larger decisions.

Though the Institute's policy-making power was concentrated in the hands of volunteers, the Institute's professional staff was not limited to performing only routine tasks. Perhaps the most important role Stewart Sheppard assumed in his early years as Institute director was as spokesman for the Institute. Before the CFA program could gain acceptance, it had to become known. Thus, Sheppard spent much of his time in 1963 and 1964 promoting the CFA charter in Federation cities. According to David Watterson, the ICFA's sixth president, the Institute owes "a great debt of gratitude to Stewart Sheppard [who] travelled the country from coast to coast visiting the local societies in the initial year and creating enthusiasm for the program." "A real salesman," in Watterson's words, Sheppard was able "to get the leaders of the various societies to enter the program in its first year." One society leader who felt it incumbent upon himself to lead the way was then-president of the Toronto Society, Leonard Barlow. Barlow, who succeeded Watterson as Institute president in 1969, calls the hiring of Sheppard "a stroke of genius"—particularly in light of his ability as a speaker. Sheppard is credited with the Institute's early success, not only for the quality of the exams that gave the CFA immediate credibility, but for his effectiveness in promoting the program.

The program experienced remarkable growth in its first five years. The 20 year debate within the National Federation no doubt helped to spark interest among the nearly 300 analysts, many of whom were Federation and industry leaders, who registered for the 1963 exam. Sheppard's efforts to gain support for the program helped solidify their interest and attract others. In 1964, the first year with a full examination schedule, the Institute expected that a number of younger Federation leaders would enter the program out of a pioneering spirit and an intention to support the new CFA. However, the turnout was greater than a spillover of Federation leadership could produce. It was indeed greater than anyone expected: 1,251 candidates for Exam I, 302 for Exam II, and 189 for Exam III—a total of 1,742, of whom 1,448 were successful. Again Stewart Sheppard deserves credit for mounting a fair and thorough series of exams, and for publicizing them through personal appearances, newspaper articles, and brochures. In 1965 the numbers again grew: 1,993 candidates took all three exams, and 1,656 passed. 1966 saw 2,010 candidates sit for the exams, with 1,513 successful, while in 1967 there were 1,693 candidates, of whom 1,410 passed. After five years, the Institute had administered nearly 8,000 tests and had awarded 1,829 charters. This was the organization that had expected to retain its Initiating Group for 10 years.

The Institute's nearly 2,000 members did not have to be accommodated in Charlottesville, but a staff to serve both them and the new registrants did. Throughout the 1960s Stewart Sheppard and Ray Smith continued to divide their time between the Institute and Virginia's Colgate Darden Graduate School of Business, theoretically devoting half of their time to each. Institute business, however, had a way of increasing exponentially and taking up one's "free" time. Ray Smith recalls spending every evening from 7 to 11 dictating responses to aspiring registrants or—at appropriate times of the year—writing to unhappy, unsuccessful candidates. Moreover, Smith personally reviewed "every single examination" after all were graded and "put them in categories for further review" by the Board of Trustees. He and Sheppard also reviewed every candidate's application and "in the early years, if there were any doubts [about eligibility]," the applications were turned over to the Admissions Committee whose recommendations were passed on to the Trustees. These daily duties, combined with Sheppard and Smith's extensive travel on behalf of the Institute, taxed the professional staff to its limit. In 1964 the Institute's support staff had been expanded to three full-time secretaries and a Recorder (i.e., registrar). In 1965 another full-time secretary was hired, and early 1966 saw the addition of a research administrator and research assistant.

Such a large staff was necessary, given the phenomenal growth of the Institute in its early years, but the space allotted to it by the Darden School was decidedly insufficient. As Stewart Sheppard recalls, "the steady evolution of the examination and research programs placed an impossible strain on Institute headquarters on the mezzanine floor of Monroe Hall." During the mid 60s Virginia's Darden School went through a period of expansion, leaving it and the Institute competing for the same office space. Sheppard and Charles Abbott found a serendipitous means for resolving these "mutual space problems." In the late summer of 1965 Abbott discovered that the William Faulkner House, which stood on several acres two miles west of the University's main grounds, was unoccupied. A large antebellum mansion surrounded with cottages and outbuildings, the house was named in honor of the novelist, who resided at Virginia from 1957 to 1959 and lectured there until his death in 1962. It had once housed a faculty club, and the University was seeking another way to utilize the space. Charles Abbott and Stewart Sheppard simultaneously decided that, subject to the approval of the Trustees, the Institute should lease Faulkner House from the University. This would provide the ever-expanding Institute with room to grow, and release some much-needed office space for the graduate business program, as well.

Initially, however, the Faulkner House and grounds would be considerably larger than the ICFA needed. Would a move there be judicious? In September 1964, a full year before the move to Faulkner House was proposed, Stewart Sheppard had noticed a shift in the air which was to prove important in the decision regarding a new location. With two sets of examinations under its belt, the Institute had solved many of its early operating problems and was becoming administratively self-sufficient. The need to create new exams, monitor grading, revise study guides, and process applications would continue—and increase—as the years went on, but by late 1964 the Institute's staff could carry out these operations smoothly.

Another challenge awaited, as Sheppard informed the Board on September 12, 1964: "The organization phase of the Institute's history being largely over, the encouragement of the writing of articles, monographs and books useful to CFA candidates and analysts generally is becoming a most important Institute activity." As Sheppard remembers it some 21 years later, the situation was more dire than the Board minutes suggest: "There was little published *for our purposes*, so we had to develop our own publications"—to serve the candidates and members, and for the benefit of the analyst community at large.

By the time the Faulkner House proposal went before the Board in September 1965, a way of fulfilling this need for specific new material had suggested itself to Stewart Sheppard, who is remembered by long-time Research and Publication chairman, Edmund Mennis, the Institute's eighth president, as a "tremendous idea man." Sheppard's "idea" was to establish at Faulkner House not only the Institute's administrative headquarters, but also a research study program. By 1970, Sheppard projected, new applications would average only 200 to

300 a year. Although the Institute's main function would continue to be the administration of exams, enrollments would level off, providing the staff with the time to administer a research program as well as a membership in need of it. On September 11, 1965, the trustees tentatively approved the move to Faulkner House and the creation of a CFA Research Foundation, whose purpose would be "to project some specific meaning to C.F.A." by developing "special projects in finance to be researched by professors and others at the expense of the C.F.A."

Three days later, Stewart Sheppard and Ray Smith met with the Institute's president, Dutton Morehouse, and with Linwood Savage, Abe Kulp, and David Williams to work out the basic format for the research foundation. According to Morehouse's notes of the meeting, it was decided to include four major areas under the program's aegis: original basic research, continuing research on industry and general topics, cooperative research with similar groups, and group seminars. In reporting on his year as Institute president in the spring of 1966, Morehouse, who was to become the CFA Research Foundation's first president, noted that on December 2, 1965, the board made its final decision to move to Faulkner House, to establish the Research Center there, and to incorporate the CFA Research Foundation. Morehouse concluded:

The basic function of the Institute is and always will be the preparation and supervision of a series of examinations looking to the professional designation of Chartered Financial Analyst. We believe, however, that we have found the answer to an ongoing program in the establishment of the Research Center of the Institute of Chartered Financial Analysts, the first center in the United States for independent research in financial analysis.

Stewart Sheppard felt that the move to Faulkner House in January 1966 might have brought the CFA Research Foundation into being "a little earlier" than otherwise anticipated. However, it began functioning soon after its establishment, overseeing a revision of Joseph Murriello's *Accounting for the Financial Analyst* in 1967, and holding its first seminar, Personal Trust Investment Management, in May of that year. The proceedings of the seminar were published as a book in 1968.

In addition to the prestige that the research seminars and publications would bring to the ICFA, the new location at the William Faulkner House had some unexpected advantages. The building and grounds added, in Sheppard's words, "an intangible feeling . . . an extra dimension of dignity to a program that was acquiring professional respectability." It also added to Abe Kulp's lore. Stewart Sheppard recalls with delight that one day "Abe Kulp was particularly gratified when two nuns appeared before his desk seeking his autograph." It was with some reluctance, Sheppard remembers, that Kulp "had to admit that he was not William Faulkner."

*   *   *

By the late 1960s, the Institute of Chartered Financial Analysts had set in place the structure that guides it to this day: the officers and trustees, the volunteer committees, the research program of seminars and publications, the admissions procedure, the exam program, and the concept of providing continuing education to Institute members. All of this had been accomplished within an orderly change in leadership. In the spring of 1964, Abe Kulp, who was to become Federation president, served his last months as president of the Institute and was succeeded by David Williams of Detroit. Williams' tenure saw the first publication of the *CFA Newsletter* in November 1964, and the first discussions of the need for the continuing education of members. In 1965, Dutton Morehouse of Chicago became ICFA president, overseeing the creation of the CFA Research Foundation (whose president he became), and the move to Faulkner House. Morehouse was followed by Linwood Savage of Boston in 1966, and Ray Hammell of New York in 1967, both of whom worked to consolidate the Institute's strength. By the time David Watterson of Cleveland assumed the ICFA presidency in 1968, the Institute was indeed finished with its "organization phase" and ready to move on to a more sophisticated understanding of its purpose.

With the achievement of such sophistication and routine, a certain sense of pioneering spirit is lost. Looking back, it is difficult to appreciate the feeling of adventure that pervaded the early years of the ICFA. Stewart Sheppard and Ray Smith, George Hansen, Dutton Morehouse, David Williams, and most of all, Abe Kulp, faced the decidedly difficult task of creating the Institute out of nothing at all. There were few models and no agreed-upon idea of what their profession entailed; yet they succeeded.

The Institute that Kulp's determination had made possible was now a self-sustaining organization. Kulp was not one to acknowledge his own importance, but others did not fail to appreciate his worth. Ray Smith expressed Kulp's contribution thus: "I worked with many great people, but the person who really stands out is Abe Kulp. He was the bulldog, the steadying force, the optimist during the times when we weren't exactly sure what we were doing." The ICFA would have many subsequent leaders who would make invaluable contributions, but to Abe Kulp it owed its very existence.

PART THREE

DEFINING THE PROFESSION

*In these days of garbage men demanding
to be called "sanitation engineers," it
seems that everyone is seeking status and
the country seems to be crawling with
people who are pretenders to
professionalism, regardless of their
occupation. I had a long talk with my
wife last night on just how she would
define a 'profession'. . . . As usual she hit
me right between the eyes with an
answer that cut brightly through the haze.
She told me that a true professional
professes to believe in something . . . that
goes beyond merely making a living. The
mere existence of these higher goals,*

whether they be healing, justice, or whatever, forces a rigid discipline upon the members of the profession as to ethics, conduct, training, talent, ability, experience, etc. This . . .leads me to ask the question whether or not we do not have some obvious goals as a profession ourselves. I suspect that they may have something to do with preserving the free market system, making capital markets efficient, or to be corny, "making capitalism work." If we do profess to believe in something that surpasses our personal interest, perhaps we are, or can become, a profession. If we don't, or if we cannot define it, maybe we should just go back to being good honest garbage men and let it go at that.

Frank E. Block
ninth ICFA President,
to George H. Norton,
admissions committee chairman,
March 2, 1967

CHAPTER FIVE
The Body of Knowledge

What constitutes a profession? For nearly two decades, the National Federation had struggled with this problem in trying to determine whether the work of the financial analyst could be considered professional. In setting up the ICFA, the Federation's leaders declared financial analysis sufficiently professional to be based—like law, medicine or accountancy—on a testable body of knowledge and an agreed-upon code of behavior.

Declaring financial analysis professional, however, did not settle the issue of how the profession was to be defined. Questions of professionalism in general continued to hound the industry's leaders. In 1966, FAF president Thomas H. Lenagh formed a Policy and Planning Committee to establish future directions for the growing Federation. In particular, the group was to study "how best . . . the Federation can assist in bringing about an internationally recognized profession of financial analysis." Chaired by William Norby, the committee commissioned leading analysts to write position papers on "whether financial analysis does qualify as a profession." Douglas Hayes, Marshall Ketchum, and Stewart Sheppard contributed papers on the subject, which were published in the November-December 1967 issue of the *Financial Analysts Journal.* Although each author defined a profession somewhat differently, they all agreed on three crucial elements of professional status: a code of ethics or professional conduct; admission to professional status attendant upon the passing of an examination; and the existence of a well-defined body of knowledge upon which such an exam is based. Ketchum felt such knowledge was primary:

> The keystone of a profession is knowledge. . . . Some professions have codes of ethics and other marks of professional status, but if an occupation is successfully to claim that it is a profession, it must convince those whom the occupation serves that it possesses knowledge and that this knowledge is useful in serving clients.

William Norby, in considering these three articles several months later, remarked that in the mind of each of the writers "there was hope that with the continued development of a common body of knowledge and a reasonably uniform methodology, coupled with further development and application of a code of ethics, professional status very possibly could be achieved in the future."

The hopes of Sheppard, Ketchum, and Hayes were vested in the Institute. The ICFA, more than any other analyst organization, served to set the standard for professional knowledge and behavior. The Federation's search for answers coincided with an Institute activity that would serve to further define the profession and advance the cause of professionalization: a compilation of the "body of knowledge."

Throughout 1967, Stewart Sheppard had become increasingly aware that the CFA examination program was in need of revision, not necessarily to increase its level of difficulty, but to improve its content. Sheppard communicated his concern to the Council of Examiners and to Edmund A. Mennis, chairman of the Research and Publications Committee. In December 1967, Mennis met with Sheppard and the council in Charlottesville to discuss their respective roles in undertaking an "intensive review" of the program. As Sheppard put it, "the Council is restricted to published study guides in formulating the 1968 series of examinations [which] prevents them in certain cases from including questions for which there are no suitable candidate study materials. . . . On the other hand, the Research and

Publications Committee needs clarification on examination objectives if it is to uncover or develop materials for new subject areas." The council based the exams on the Study Guides, which were themselves based on the exams.

Recognizing the "broad policy issues" underlying this dilemma and the need to step back and look at the examinations as a whole, the group recommended to Institute president Raymond Hammell that an ad hoc policy committee be formed to review the entire program and the respective areas of research and examination. Hammell approved and appointed a committee consisting of himself and David Watterson (representing the Trustees), Ed Mennis and Frank Block (representing the Research and Publications Committee) and Gilbert Palmer and Joseph Glibert (representing the Council of Examiners).

Initially, the main burden of reviewing the CFA program fell to the Research and Publication Committee, which held its first face-to-face meeting in January 1968 under the chairmanship of Ed Mennis. Since the Examiners were to construct exams based on material recommended by the Research and Publications Committee, it was incumbent upon the latter group to completely review the existing structure. The previous year, the committee had been subdivided according to four subject areas: accounting, economics, financial analysis, and portfolio management. To meet the needs of the exam review, two further subdivisions took place in early 1968: ethical standards and the organization of a research department.

The 1968 Research and Publications Committee was particularly well suited to its task. In addition to such academic stalwarts as Henry Latane and Leo Stone, the committee included a wide variety of experienced practitioners such as Dutton Morehouse. Morehouse's influence on the committee extended beyond his presence. As president of the Institute in 1965, he had appointed three of the *Financial Analysts Journal* staff to the Research and Publications Committee, "to avoid conflicts of interest between the *Journal* and the Institute. . . . " Thus, not only were associate editors Frank Block and Ed Mennis available to help reformulate the body of knowledge, but also the *Journal's* editor, Nicholas Molodovsky, universally acknowledged as one of the leading thinkers in financial analysis.

Molodovsky served from 1964 to 1969 as editor and publisher of the *Financial Analysts Journal*, which he transformed, in the words of Robert Milne, from a "trade association publication with some signs of promise to its present position as the authoritative journal of the profession with a worldwide readership and reputation." Molodovsky consistently exhorted analysts to familiarize themselves with the newly developed quantitative techniques lest they "become illiterate in their own field." He imparted to the *Journal* a pedagogic function by—in Mennis' words—introducing "articles by leading academics to get the profession familiar with the work in the academic community that challenged the very foundations of financial analysis." Later in 1968, in recognition of Molodovsky's contributions, the FAF established in his name its highest award, bestowed on individuals whose contributions have been "of such significance as to change the direction of the profession. . . . "

To Molodovsky fell the task of coordinating the subcommittee on financial analysis, whose part in the Institute's comprehensive exam review was to evaluate the program as it related to analysis as a whole. The rest of the examination material was subdivided by subject. Mennis, the Research and Publications chairman, coordinated the areas of ethics and research department organization; David Norr of New York was responsible for accounting; Dutton Morehouse oversaw economics; and Frank Block chaired the portfolio management subcommittee. The various subcommittees worked throughout the late winter and early spring of 1968, reviewing the Institute's entire examination program to determine whether the examination materials were comprehensive, suitable, and placed at the appropriate exam level.

On May 5, 1968, Mennis informed the Board of Trustees that the subcommittees' various reports were essentially complete, though not yet coordinated into one coherent plan. The reports constituted a major rethinking of the Institute's program. For the Institute in particular and the industry as a whole, the committee's work defined the "body of knowledge" on which financial analysis would be based.

The subcommittees proposed many changes in the examination structure. Perhaps most commonly recommended was the transfer of subject matter from one examination level to another. The nature of financial analysis was changing. The knowledge base necessary for a Level I candidate in 1969 was already different from what he or she would have been tested on at the Institute's beginning. For example, Edmund Mennis suggested that testing on the topic of research department organization and administration be discontinued as outdated. Reasoning that many candidates now came from smaller organizations and were more likely "to depend on a few consultants to provide specific services" than to fund extensive research departments, Mennis concluded that candidates' study time "could be more profitably devoted to other areas of greater importance."

Two of the subcommittees, financial analysis and portfolio management, proposed significant additions to the examination program. Noting that "Examination I is extremely weak in presenting the elements of portfolio management," Frank Block suggested that more be demanded of entering candidates, specifically that "the young security analyst [learn] to think in terms of the characteristics of securities first, and then to begin the application of his reasoning powers to questions of value, price, timing and security usage." He also recommended that portfolio construction be included on Examination I.

Molodovsky's financial analysis subcommittee would increase the scope of the examinations even further. Not surprisingly, it recommended that the candidates' understanding of quantitative techniques—specifically, statistical analysis—be increased and "severely tested in Examination I," and that Examination III include questions on the quantitative techniques of portfolio management and computer applications. In addition, Molodovsky proposed "to enlarge the curriculum of the C.F.A. examinations by introducing the subjects of the history and structure of business corporations, separation of ownership and control, of the nature and of investment effects of corporate mergers, of antitrust policy and of economic concentration." Such knowledge was assumed to be so vital as to be a prerequisite to entering the program.

In May, the subcommittees' reports were submitted by Mennis to the trustees, the Council of Examiners, and the entire Research and Publications Committee for comments. Their reactions were to be evaluated by the ad hoc committee for CFA Examination Content, whose "final planning document rather than the subcommittee reports," according to Mennis, would be the foundation "on which future action will be based." In August 1968, Mennis sent the ad hoc committee a summary report he had prepared on the Research and Publications Committee's finalized work. He also outlined for them the four areas of controversy remaining after comments had been received from the trustees and others: (1) Should the operation of a research department be retained as an examination subject? (2) Should technical and market analysis be included? (3) Should senior industry specialists be given advanced testing in security analysis rather than portfolio management? (4) Should an extensive background in the history of economic and social change, business corporations, and economic institutions be required of entering candidates? All of these propositions were rejected.

With the ad hoc committee's final recommendations, the scheme for redefining the program was formalized. Mennis' August report had spelled out in considerable detail both the program prerequisites and the specific knowledge of economics, ethical standards, accounting, financial analysis, and portfolio management required for each examination. This became the Institute's Basic Planning Document, upon which subsequent exam revisions were based. At the same time, Stewart Sheppard prepared a General Topic Outline for candidates, enabling them to see the specific subject matter of each exam.

The comprehensiveness of the 1968 committee work is best illustrated by comparing the description of required exam topics which appeared in the 1968 CFA brochure (Exhibit I) with that appearing as the General Topic Outline in the 1969 brochure (Exhibit II). The generalized list of subject areas was transformed, through the committee's exam review work, into a detailed outline of the knowledge required to earn the CFA designation. The concepts of a Basic Planning Document (Appendix B) and General Topic Outline continue to be used by the Institute today, with the latter printed in each annual Study Guide. The content of each has changed several times—including an extensive revision in 1975—to reflect the dynamic nature of the body of knowledge on which financial analysis is based.

*   *   *

Once the Basic Planning Document and General Topic Outline had been composed and could serve as graphic representations of the CFA Program, the Research and Publications Committee, still headed by Ed Mennis, undertook the enormous task of reviewing the existing study materials for each exam to determine how well they corresponded to the recently defined body of knowledge. To avoid abrupt changes in the program, it was decided that the job would be spread out over several years. The committee first concentrated on Exam I, so that its revision could be complete for 1970. This would not, Mennis cautioned, preclude modifications in the other exams; rather, it would indicate that "the major effort each year be on a different exam."

To assist the committee in their work, the Institute staff sorted through the recommended readings in the study guides, textbooks, and CFA publications and classified them according to each topic in the planning document. Research assistant Gerald MacFarlane, who had joined the staff in 1967, was responsible for this task. He subsequently coordinated the committee's review of existing materials with the preparation of upcoming study guides. In addition to MacFarlane's work, the Institute was drawing on the services of a librarian to prepare bibliographies on each exam subject area. According to Edmund Mennis, this enabled committee members to "devote their efforts to reviewing articles rather than seeking them out."

MacFarlane's compilation of study material was sent to the committee members in November 1968. The five area coordinators (Mennis, Molodovsky, Block, Morehouse and Robert Ellis) divided the material among their subcommittee members for evaluation in terms of its suitability, its potential duplication of other readings, and its appropriate placement at a particular exam level. The reviewers would also consider whether additional or substitute material was needed for a given topic, and determine where gaps existed, so that new material could be sought out or commissioned.

The literature review continued through the spring of 1969. Each article and book was evaluated by an appropriate committee member, subcommittee coordinator and Research and Publications Chairman Mennis. During the summer new material was circulated, with the aim of completing a second edition of *CFA Readings in Financial Analysis* and the 1970 Study Guides by the fall. The work proceeded smoothly, despite the geographical scattering of committee members and the sudden loss of Nicholas Molodovsky, who died in March 1969.

The enormous attention to detail required by the exam and literature reviews of 1968 and 1969 was not without potential hazards. In commenting on the initial exam review, Trustee Douglas Hayes noted that a "general problem may have arisen from making the committee assignments along topical lines . . . [for] there was a tendency to recommend that each topic receive some coverage in all of the examinations. . . . " Hayes worried that too great an increase in the scope of each examination might lead to "less penetrating questions" on each topic. The ad hoc committee had no doubt taken this into account in rejecting some of the proposed additions.

A similar problem arose in the literature review. In their zeal to update and supplement existing material, the committee members ran the risk of overburdening candidates. In May 1969, Gerald MacFarlane expressed his concern on this matter to Ed Mennis. Stressing the need for balance among the three exams, MacFarlane feared that Examination I was becoming too complex and that they might "be expecting too much" of the candidates. Mennis had had a parallel concern: "I agree that we may be putting an undue burden of reading on the candidates for Exam I and we may also be getting out of proportion with respect to the II and III Exams as well." For this reason, Mennis suggested that they "sit down and take a look at the package as a whole. . . . [I]t may well be that in the final review we may do some further shifting around. . . . "

In May 1969, Mennis summarized the committee's work-in-progress for Institute president David Watterson and the trustees, and acknowledged that the work done by Molodovsky, Block, and the others was impressive. Yet he felt the task was still several years from completion. In a sense he underestimated, for defining—and redefining—the body of knowledge on which financial analysis is based is a never-ending task.

*   *   *

The work of the Research and Publications Committee in the late 1960s served another important function: it uncovered those areas in which further research was needed to supplement existing knowledge. The primary lack of information was in the area of portfolio management. As Mennis points out, "it is hard to remember now, with all of the literature pouring out from the universities and the profession, [but] back then very little was available to be used as basis for exam questions on portfolio management."

In order to fill this gap in the available literature, the Institute commissioned the CFA Research Foundation to sponsor a series of seminars on portfolio management. The proceedings of the first seminar, Personal Trust Investment Management—held at Faulkner House in May 1967—were edited by Frank Block, who explained the choice of personal trust by noting that "very little of merit has been written on the subject of trust investing. The typical investment textbook devotes perhaps a paragraph, or a page or so, to the subject." Moreover, much of what had been written reflected the outdated philosophy of buying only "good old bonds," rather than the considerably more diverse approaches recommended by the experts, who included Block, Mennis, and Joseph Y. Jeanes of the Research and Publications Committee, as well as M. Harvey Earp, James Close, C. Roderick O'Neil and Institute "godfathers" Dutton Morehouse and Linwood Savage, among others. The resulting debate added much to the existing literature, especially in the area of ethics. It was included as a reading for Exam III in 1969.

Acting on the work done by the Research and Publications Committee, the CFA Research Foundation sponsored three subsequent seminars to generate additional material on portfolio management. In September 1968, Esmond Gardner chaired a seminar on pension fund investment management; in May 1969 Andrew Feretti conducted a program on investment company portfolio management; in May 1970 the last of the series, a seminar on property and liability insurance investment management, was chaired by Samuel B. Jones. One year after each seminar was held, its proceedings were published in book form. Thus, by 1971 there were four books on specific areas of portfolio management where only scattered pages had existed before.

In August 1971, Richard D. Irwin published a volume that filled an equally important gap in the financial literature: *Quantitative Techniques for Financial Analysis*, by Jerome L. Valentine and Edmund A. Mennis. This text, sponsored by the Research Foundation and posthumously dedicated to Nicholas Molodovsky, was funded in part by monies that Molodovsky had donated upon receiving the FAF award that bore his name. The book was intended to help correct a situation about which Molodovsky had long been concerned: unless analysts learned quantitative techniques and computer applications, they ran the risk of becoming "illiterate in their own field."

Recalling the circumstances that led to the writing of this volume, Mennis noted that originally, CFA candidates "were older and were in many instances far removed from academic exposure to modern statistical techniques and the use of the computer." They were not inclined to return to the classroom to learn these techniques. Thus, said Mennis:

> What we needed was a book that presumed little background in quantitative techniques by the reader, that was oriented to problems in financial analysis, and that dealt more with selection of the appropriate technique, the input, the output and how it was interpreted rather than the detailed mechanics of a particular technique.

Finding no such book in the literature, Mennis, then senior vice president of the Trust Investment Division of Republic National Bank of Dallas, offered to work with Valentine, who headed computer applications in Mennis' division. As Stewart Sheppard noted in an introduction to Quantitative Techniques, their collaboration was no ordinary "joint authorship." Instead, "Mr. Valentine assumed the responsibility of organizing and writing the text [while] Dr. Mennis reviewed the innumerable drafts . . . from the viewpoint of a practicing analyst who was some years removed from academic exposure to quantitative techniques and who had only a nodding acquaintance with the computer." Or, as Mennis put it, "Jerry wrote the text until I could understand it—and every chapter was rewritten many, many times!"

Once completed, the book was rushed out in a pre-publication edition to make it available for 1970 candidates; it was officially published the following summer. Initially distributed free despite the Institute's budget worries, *Quantitative Techniques*, after several printings and one revision, became a good source of revenue for the Foundation, because the authors took no payment. Its publication marked another step forward in filling the gaps in the analyst's professional literature.

*   *   *

In April 1970, Leonard Barlow of Toronto, reporting to Institute members on his year as ICFA president, took the time to commend Ed Mennis and his committee for their extensive work in reappraising the CFA course material. During Barlow's notably active presidency, the restructuring of the CFA exams had been essentially completed; however, Barlow noted one further element that underscored the need to revise the CFA program. The CFA population had changed considerably since the program's inception: " . . . in 1965, approximately 78 percent of those obtaining their CFAs were over 50 years of age." But by the end of the decade, with younger analysts entering the program, "approximately 74 percent of those obtaining CFAs in 1969 were under 50 years of age and of these, 45 percent were under 40 years of age." Barlow observed that such analysts brought a less traditional outlook to their work. They also brought different academic training and different expectations into the Institute. Financial analysis was undergoing a major shift and the Research and Publications Committee's work in the late 1960s was an attempt to keep the CFA program current with these changes.

The examination and literature review undertaken by the Institute was an essential step for the profession of financial analysis. It addressed the crucial element which can validate any pretensions to professionalism: the existence of a testable body of knowledge.

CHAPTER SIX
Ethics and Standards

The Institute's work from 1968 to 1970 was carried out against a backdrop of difficult circumstances in Charlottesville. Early in 1968, George Hansen, one of the Institute's founding fathers and its long-time treasurer, announced his intended retirement from a position he had held since 1956—executive secretary of the Financial Analysts Federation. At the same time, the Institute's executive director, Stewart Sheppard, had begun to contemplate career changes, having received offers of full-time academic posts at other universities. With the Institute's administration functioning smoothly, Sheppard was ready to take on new challenges; yet he was reluctant to sever relations with the analyst community. Aware of Hansen's plans, Sheppard expressed to FAF president Robert H. Perry his interest in assuming the post of executive secretary at the Federation. He proposed combining the duties of that office with his duties as ICFA director; he would conduct business from Federation headquarters in New York, but return to Charlottesville several days each week to oversee operations there.

Perry referred Sheppard's proposal to the Federation's Policy and Planning Committee, under William Norby. They found a number of advantages in having Sheppard fill the upcoming vacancy, citing in particular his "outstanding administrative record in building and developing the C.F.A. program," his exceptional skills as a communicator, and his educational background. The committee also looked favorably upon the opportunity to share Sheppard's salary expenses with the Institute, and even more important, upon the cohesion that Sheppard's shared services would promote between the ICFA and FAF. As Perry put it, "Stewart Sheppard's supervision of the administrative programs of both the Federation and the Institute represents a strong step toward bringing these two organizations closer and welding them together." Sheppard himself recalls that his basic intent in proposing to fill the Federation's position was to strengthen ties between the two organizations.

Sheppard's proposal was accepted, and in the summer of 1968 he moved his office to New York City, preparing to assume Hansen's duties. Though Sheppard frequently returned to Charlottesville, and conducted Institute business from his New York office, his absence was felt at Faulkner House. Ray Smith, Sheppard's original assistant and by 1968, administrative director for the Institute, took responsibility for the day-to-day functioning of the Institute. Smith had intended 1968 to be his last year at the ICFA, planning to teach full time at the Darden School beginning with the upcoming fall semester, but postponed his departure in light of Sheppard's new duties.

Smith was aided in his task by a woman who is remembered as one of the Institute's most stalwart employees. From her initial employment in 1966 to her retirement in 1977, Beatrice Gordon served the ICFA as a tireless staff member who, in Ray Smith's words, "turned out an incredible amount of work." In her capacity as Institute recorder, Gordon took care of the Institute's main business, handling candidate registration, fee processing, and study group liaison. As her role at the Institute grew, and particularly during Stewart Sheppard's years in New York, Gordon also acted as coordinator in Charlottesville for the Institute's various committees. Leonard Barlow, whose tenure as Institute president from 1969 to 1970 coincided with much of Sheppard's Federation employment, recalls Beatrice Gordon's devotion to the Institute with particular gratitude, remembering her acting "almost as Den Mother" to the trustees, graders, and various committee members who visited Charlottesville on Institute business.

Though Sheppard's physical removal from the Institute's daily operation caused hardships for the staff in Charlottesville, Sheppard himself was by no means uninvolved in Institute policy. As mentioned previously, the exam review and its attendant committee work had been undertaken on Sheppard's initiative. In addition, Sheppard continued to be zealous in his concern for the ethical standards of the Institute. As early as 1964, when he was still busy promoting the fledgling Institute, Sheppard had delivered a speech before the Southwestern Finance Association in Dallas entitled, "The Professionalization of the Financial Analyst." In it, Sheppard had agreed that the "moral element" of a profession "is of equal importance" with "the mastery of a complex intellectual discipline." Three years later, in a *Financial Analysts Journal* article of the same title (though different content), Sheppard again emphasized the ethical aspect of financial analysis, asserting that investors were entitled to some "public warranty" that those they entrusted with the resources were "individuals possessed not only with technical competency but also with a moral and ethical sense of responsibility." Along with David Watterson, Sheppard had been instrumental in formulating the Institute's Code of Ethics, on which this "sense of responsibility" was to rest.

As the Institute's program developed throughout the late 1960s, however, it became apparent to the trustees and administrators that the guidelines needed updating and further clarification. In 1967, Institute president Linwood Savage called upon the Professional Ethics Committee to work on overall revision of the guidelines and code. The 1967 chairman, M. Mallory Gray, reported to the trustees later that year that the task had proven too large to handle by mail and that "this Committee has been active throughout the year but seems to have been spinning its wheels in the sand most of the time." The difficulty of clarifying ethical conduct had been forseen by Stewart Sheppard, who had warned Gray that "we must be reconciled to the fact that we shall have to go through an initial period of even fuzzy thinking."

Sheppard's parallel employment with the ICFA and FAF in the late 1960s put him in a unique position to oversee work on ethical standards revision, for from 1967 to 1970 the two organizations sponsored a joint Ethical Standard Committee. Also particularly active during this period of clarification was John G. Gillis of Boston's Hill and Barlow law firm, who acted as joint counsel to the Federation and the Institute. Gillis was able to specify the legal differences between the two entities as they applied to ethics. He surveyed the enforcement procedures of other professions, notably law, architecture, and accounting, and conveyed his findings to Sheppard and Carl L.A. Beckers of St. Louis, the joint committee's guiding light during those years.

The work of revising and clarifying the Code of Ethics and Guidelines was undertaken with a view towards enforcement. The Ethics Committee had looked into a few possible ethics violations during the first four years of its existence, but those were primarily concerned with cases of "flamboyant advertising." No full scale investigations had been held, nor did any explicit procedure exist for conducting them. Increasingly, the Institute officers and administrators worried about this gap, particularly in the late 1960s, when the financial industry was troubled by instances of insider information abuse. In December 1968, Ethics Committee member Jay Vawter had undertaken an extensive revision of the Institute's code and guidelines, at the urging of committee chairman Beckers. Vawter, new to the committee at the time, remembers being surprised to have Beckers suggest that he "take a shot at rewriting the CFA code." Intending to achieve greater specificity, Vawter wanted to separate the code (which was a "loose statement of principles") from the detailed guidelines. In light of current market conditions, Vawter had even included a new guideline dealing entirely with inside information.

Between the winter of 1968 and the fall of 1970, extensive redrafting of the Institute's and Federation's Codes of Ethics and their respective guidelines was carried out as a first step on the road to enforcement. Essentially, two groups were involved: the joint Professional Ethics Committee, chaired by Carl Beckers with the legal counsel of John Gillis, and a special ICFA committee, appointed by Institute president David Watterson in December 1968, and consisting of Leonard Barlow — who acted as committee chairman — George S. Bissell, Frank Block, and Douglas Hayes. This latter committee was to recommend to the ICFA trustees who should be responsible for reviewing and updating ethical standards and guidelines; initiating and carrying out investigations into alleged breaches of conduct; and, finally, hearing and adjudicating alleged offenses, including the imposition of penalties where guilt was determined.

In January 1969, Leonard Barlow sent a comprehensive "Aide Memoire" to David Watterson, Stewart Sheppard, and the members of the special committee, in which he detailed the "elaborate arrangements and procedures" that had evolved in the legal, accounting, and architectural professions for investigating and adjudicating ethical violations. Barlow noted in particular that for law and accounting "the function of supervising their ethical codes is clearly divided into two parts — a legislative and interpretive function, and a quasi-judicial function." By comparison, Barlow pointed out, "the By-Laws of the Institute of Chartered Financial Analysts dealing with the establishment and enforcement of its Code of Ethics appear to be quite inadequate and probably should be improved."

In fact, at that time the bylaws contained no specific means for investigating, hearing, or imposing penalties on members alleged to have violated the code. If the Institute was to benefit from the experience of other professional organizations, several changes were in order. The Ethics Committee first needed to complete its work of revising the code and guidelines for greater specificity, at the same time assuming for itself the power "to entertain complaints and investigate alleged infractions." Further, the Board of Trustees needed to create a new committee "empowered to hear and adjudicate alleged offenses . . . and recommend penalties. . . . " Finally, well-defined and graduated penalties had to be determined for those found to be in violation of the Institute's Code.

The joint Ethical Standards Committee already had begun to attend to those changes. Based on the work of John Gillis and Leonard Barlow, Beckers's committee recognized early on the need to emulate the disciplinary procedures of other professions, particularly regarding the formation of two committees—one "legislative," the other "judicial"—to handle the investigation and prosecution of ethics charges. As early as February 1969, John Gillis had drafted proposed revisions of the code and a new set of guidelines (to be called "Standards of Professional Conduct"), expanding them from the 7 adopted in 1964 to 12. Specific standards were developed to deal with full disclosure of firm or individual interest in securities recommended, full disclosure of any conflict of interest, and objectivity and accuracy. Also new was a standard on informing one's employer of the "existence and content" of the ICFA Code and Standards, on revealing the sources of one's compensation, and the trustees' powers of charter revocation.

*   *   *

As Carl Beckers remembers it, the thrust behind these and the subsequent, finalized code, guideline, and bylaw revisions presented to the trustees in 1969 was an "unmitigated desire to self regulate." Problems regarding insider information and corporate disclosure within the financial community served to intensify the Institute's need to act, lest an outside agency preempt its powers of self-regulation. The ICFA was, as Frank Block wrote to Leonard Barlow in the spring of 1969, engaged in a sincere effort "to do something rather than just talk about doing something."

The trustees and committee members believed that, as Beckers recalls, "we should pattern our efforts to regulate ourselves on the case method"—that the guidelines (standards) should be set and publicized, and then each case interpreted in light of the standards, much as our legal system functions. As a result of this aim, Beckers's committee submitted proposed bylaw revisions, drafted by John Gillis, that served to broaden the powers of the Ethical Standards Committee—which was renamed the Professional Ethics Committee—and to establish a Professional Grievances Committee (renamed the Professional Conduct Committee in 1976). The former, chaired by Beckers, was to develop, amend, and interpret standards for trustees and members; the latter, chaired by Austin Hume, to formulate methods of enforcing Standards and to conduct investigations, hold hearings and report its recommendations to the board—for disciplinary action where necessary. The ICFA now had its legislative and judicial committees.

In addition to revising the Code of Ethics, expanding the Standards, and establishing the respective ethics and grievance committees, Beckers and Gillis also devised "Rules of Procedure" to be followed in the event of an ethics prosecution. Acting on the experience of other professions, the Institute included in its rules a provision for establishing regional grievance committees to investigate and hear complaints on the local level first. Such regionalization was of obvious importance to the Federation as well as the Institute. However, at the Federation Delegates Meeting in May 1969, the revisions respective to the Federation were subject to "spirited discussion" which indicated to Beckers "the need for further deliberation."

The ICFA trustees who, given their direct relationship to members (rather than Societies) could more readily act with one mind, unanimously approved the revised code and new procedures on May 12, 1969. Institute members were informed of the changes in the November 12, 1969 CFA Newsletter, which printed the new Code of Ethics, Standards of Professional Conduct, and Rules of Procedure in their entirety. The 1970-71 CFA Program brochure, sent to candidates the following year, contained the same material. These developments, as Beckers had written to his committee, were a major step forward, permitting the Institute "to govern the conduct of any Chartered Financial Analyst."

However, one side effect of putting standards and procedures in place is that any inherent problems become apparent almost immediately. Our legal system—be it on national, state, or institutional level—is subject to continual modification both by legislative action and judicial interpretation. As soon as the Institute's procedures had been spelled out and adopted, thoughtful members began to notice flaws. In the fall of 1969, the new ICFA president, Leonard Barlow, wrote to Carl Beckers and Stewart Sheppard, wondering whether the procedures didn't leave too much discretionary responsibility "for determining whether a complaint should be investigated" in the hands of the executive director and president. Barlow suggested that either the Professional Ethics or Grievances Committee act in an advisory capacity in these matters. Barlow, Sheppard, Gillis, and Beckers worked on these procedures throughout the fall.

Another potential problem area was the annual questionnaire sent to members. Since its inception, the Institute had required of its candidates a signed statement indicating that they understood that failure to comply with the Institute's code and guidelines could result in the revocation of any charter attained. In 1968, the joint Ethics Committee chaired by Horace Buxton had come up with an affidavit to be sent to all current members (not only candidates) testifying that their professional behavior was in compliance with the Institute's standards. Sheppard had incorporated this into the ICFA's directory information questionnaire that same year.

But as Ed Mennis, vice president of the Institute under Leonard Barlow, noted, by 1969-70 it had become clear that "the wording of the questionnaire" was a problem. Sheppard began work on revising the annual ethics questionnaire in October 1969. Rewording proved to be difficult. Originally Institute members had been asked to consider the following:

Has your professional financial conduct ever been under criticism by a court, public official, business or professional organization?

As Sheppard interpreted it, the central uncertainty with the question lay in "a possible prejudgement factor implied in the use of the word 'criticism'." Moreover, "charges of unethical conduct brought by a customer or client" appeared not to need reporting by the CFA respondent. As committeeman Charles Berents noted, "the main point is to write the question so that there cannot be concealment of material evidence or fact. It is essentially an alerting process." With this in mind, Sheppard and John Gillis drafted a new two-part question. The first part questioned the CFA concerning complaints against his or her business or professional conduct, while the second concerned actual inquiries or proceedings. These considerably more specific questions were accepted by the trustees in September 1970, and incorporated into that year's candidate and member forms.

Even as the work of refining the wording of code, standards, and administrative procedures was being finalized, the Institute officers and committee members were engaged in bringing the issue of professional ethics to the attention of the membership at large. The focus of their efforts was the ICFA's Annual Meeting in Dallas, April 26, 1970. There a panel discussion was presented "on ethical problems relating to financial practices." The panel was chaired by Carl Beckers and included George Bissell, John Gillis, David Watterson and incoming Institute president, Edmund Mennis. Beckers, Gillis, and Stewart Sheppard had written up four hypothetical situations involving ethical decisions in business practices which were circulated among ICFA members and discussed by the panel in Dallas. Of special interest were the case situations relating to conflicts of interest and use of insider information, matters of much concern to the financial community. In discussing the various situations, the Institute's panel was careful to identify the appropriate Standard of Professional Conduct that applied to each case. The panel was judged a considerable success.

As a follow-up to the Dallas meeting, and in an effort to reach CFAs who had not attended, the Institute reprinted the ethics situations in the July 7, 1970 *CFA Newsletter*. Individual CFAs were requested to respond, outlining what they would do in the hypothetical situations, and which specific principles of the code and guidelines were applicable. The responses were to be incorporated into a planned article on the entire proceedings for the *Financial Analysts Journal*.

Coordinating these responses was Stewart Sheppard, who returned to Charlottesville in the summer of 1970. Though Sheppard had made considerable efforts to balance his FAF and ICFA responsibilities, the Institute's staff and officers felt the lack of his presence on the scene. Moreover, Sheppard's availability had been encroached upon when he had been asked to assume the editorship of the *Financial Analysts Journal*, following the sudden death of Nicholas Molodovsky in the spring of 1969. Although this appointment was only temporary (at the end of 1969 Jack L. Treynor took over the editorship), it was perceived as a further hardship by Institute officers and staff alike. Early in 1970, Sheppard was approached with what he recalls as "an ultimatum" from David Watterson, Leonard Barlow, and Ed Mennis—the Institute's past, present, and incoming presidents. Still firm in his desire to foster close ties between the Institute and Federation, Sheppard nonetheless realized his first loyalty was to the ICFA, whose current status he had done so much to foster. Consequently, Sheppard resigned from his position as executive secretary of the Federation and resumed his "full time" duties in Charlottesville on July 1, 1970. According to Ed Mennis, Sheppard's return had an immediate impact "on the renewed vigor of the Institute's activities."

Throughout the summer and early fall of 1970, Sheppard compiled the analysts' responses and supervised the transcription and editing of the Dallas meeting with the help of Carl Beckers. Beckers and Ethics Committee member Tom Mathers assumed responsibility for the proposed *FAJ* article. Unfortunately, the material proved recalcitrant, and no article was ever published. However, the Dallas panel discussion had been taped and was available for use, and the Institute continued its efforts to educate members about ethical issues by holding other panels.

*   *   *

In February 1971, Carl Beckers addressed the St. Louis Society of Financial Analysts about the Institute's revised code and new standards. Beckers examined the motives behind the creation of such documents. The ICFA trustees and administrators, he said, "recognized that there was a need for us to *exercise and demonstrate* to others a self-discipline in an industry that today is so vitally engaged with management of investment funds and savings throughout the United States and even the world." Indeed Barlow, Mennis, Sheppard, and Beckers, and the many others who worked to improve the Institute's code and standards and to set in place grievance procedures recognized only too clearly that the Institute must move swiftly and decisively in the area of ethical enforcement, lest its powers of self-regulation be usurped by an outside agency.

Though there would be a continuing need to assert this self-regulatory authority throughout the 1970s, the work of the Institute's officers and its Professional Ethics Committee in the late 1960s provided the basis for maintaining self-regulation. In 1968, when the Ethical Standards Committee began its review of the Code and Guidelines, the Institute had essentially no procedures established to investigate ethical violations by its members. By the end of Ed Mennis' second term as ICFA president in 1972, however, the Institute had a revised Code, expanded Standards, a Professional Grievances Committee with ten regional subcommittees (established in 1971), published Rules of Procedure, and several cases under review. Indeed, the ICFA had "exercised and demonstrated" the firmness of its commitment to self-discipline and self-regulation.

CHAPTER SEVEN
Consolidating Gains

On May 22, 1972, Edmund Mennis marked the end of his second term as Institute president by reporting to the membership on the year's work. It had been a busy year. The drive toward greater professionalism that had resulted in a revised examination structure, a newly delineated body of knowledge, and a greatly strengthened ethical enforcement program had been time-consuming as well as productive.

This work had taken place during the administrations of three particularly active board presidents—David Watterson (1968-69), Leonard Barlow (1969-70), and Mennis himself, who had been asked and agreed to serve two terms (1970-72) in order to provide continuity of leadership during Stewart Sheppard's return to Charlottesville. While the Institute's previous leaders were by no means inactive, their energies had been devoted primarily to organizing the examination program and to administrative procedures. By the time David Watterson took over in the summer of 1968, however, the ICFA was ready to begin reappraising its activities. In Watterson, Barlow, and Mennis, the Institute found leaders who were willing—and determined—to do the job.

Under Watterson, the Institute had tackled its extensive reevaluation of the examination program and conducted a detailed review of the reading materials available to candidates.

His tenure had also seen the CFA Research Foundation become increasingly active, publishing its first seminar monograph in August 1968, and holding its second seminar in portfolio management in December of that year. Organizationally and financially independent, the Research Foundation was nevertheless very closely aligned with the Institute at that time, holding its seminars at Faulkner House and utilizing Stewart Sheppard, Ray Smith, and Gerald MacFarlane of the ICFA staff. Moreover, Watterson himself was keenly interested in the Foundation's activities. In fact, in 1971 Watterson succeeded Dutton Morehouse as president of the Research Foundation—a capacity in which he served until 1975—and was made an *ex officio* trustee of the Institute.

Watterson's presidency also saw considerable work done by the Institute's Admissions Committee. Commissioned in the Bylaws with the task of resolving disputed candidacies, this committee furthered the Institute's efforts towards professionalization by determining whether potential candidates were sufficiently engaged in the practice of financial analysis to be admitted to the CFA program. Although practitioners were readily identifiable in other professions, it was not always clear whether or not a given candidate could actually be considered a financial analyst. Most of the day-to-day decisions regarding applicants could be made by Ray Smith, but some candidates fell into disputed areas— especially regarding relevant employment or experience— and were referred by Smith or Beatrice Gordon to the committee.

While the Admissions Committee did not set policy regarding standards of eligibility (that was the purview of the trustees), its decisions functioned as a kind of interpretive guideline on what the work of an analyst was, and what it was not. Beginning with a seminal meeting chaired by George Norton in May 1968, and continuing through the chairmanships of Louis Whitehead and Mary Petrie (1970-72), the committee reevaluated general experience categories. During these years, changes were occuring in the profession as a whole, and acceptable candidate employment had to take account of these changes. In the late 1960s, for example, the committee had to decide whether candidates who were chartists or technicians qualified for the program. They also judged whether the Institute should admit those whose entire experience was in portfolio management, those who worked in mergers and acquisitions, and those who were corporate officials investing working capital in short term funds. Several of these categories would continue to be scrutinized by the committee and the trustees for many years; some that were unacceptable in 1968 became acceptable employment categories later.

By 1970, however, conditions in the industry were becoming so troublesome that the committee's main focus became current employment rather than simply acceptable employment. The Admissions Committee and the Board of Trustees alike recognized that many CFA candidates might be "unemployed involuntarily" before completion of the program. While the Board was willing to allow unemployed candidates to continue the examination process, receipt of a charter remained contingent upon being employed "under an official Institute employment category."

In May 1969, his closing year as president, David Watterson applauded the accomplishments of the various Institute committees. Through their efforts, the "early challenge of objectively testing [the] analytical abilities" of suitable candidates had been met, "largely through a continuing process of upgrading examination contents and study materials."

Watterson's successor, Leonard Barlow, saw the first implementation of the revised examination structure during his year of office. Perhaps coincidentally, failure rates on the exams had begun to rise. Although the examinations were more rigorous in the sense of being more comprehensive, the probable cause of the increase in failed exams was the comparative lack of experience of entering candidates. With the 1969 examination, admissions under the "grandfather clause" devised at the Institute's beginnings were terminated. CFA candidates were younger now, with fewer years in the business. To ensure their adequate preparation, Barlow appointed a committee under the chairmanship of Trustee James A. Close, to examine and suggest ways of improving the existing study group structure within local societies and at colleges. The aim was to have the Institute work more closely with study group sponsors to raise the level of their functioning, just as the content of the exams and study materials had been improved significantly in recent years.

In addition to the Institute's efforts to better serve candidates, the end of Leonard Barlow's presidency and the first year of Ed Mennis's also saw attempts made to serve members' needs by attending to their "continuing education." The CFA Research Foundation continued to sponsor seminars on topics of interest to CFAs; the Institute sent the proceedings of these seminars free of charge to members. At the same time, the Institute was beginning to develop a plan for providing other materials to its nearly 2,500 charterholders. Perhaps the most significant development in "continuing education" was the creation of the *CFA Digest* in 1969.

The *Digest* had an interesting history. The idea of publishing abstracted articles occurred to Stewart Sheppard in the very early days of the ICFA, for he is quoted in the minutes of the September 19, 1963, Board of Trustees' meeting as suggesting that the Institute's education program be supplemented by "a digest of books and articles on a regular publication basis." Sheppard's idea was not pursued then, which is not surprising; at the time it was proposed, the Institute was awarding its first charters and had yet to give a full series of examinations.

The suggestion did not die, however. Three years later, in the spring of 1966, there were rumors—particularly at the Federation in New York—that the Institute was going to publish a quarterly digest which would, in effect, compete with the *Financial Analysts Journal.* The source of this speculation was an item from the February 4, 1966, *CFA Newsletter* which indicated that in pursuing its goal of continuing education for members, the Institute's Research Center at Faulkner House would "publish quarterly a *CFA Digest* which would abstract a wide range of articles of interest to financial analysts." Although the *Newsletter* contained the assurance that the "proposed *CFA Digest* would in no way conflict with our present *Financial Analysts Journal*," the editorial board of the *Journal* was not convinced.

One month later, Federation president Thomas Lenaugh was corresponding with Steward Sheppard and Institute president Dutton Morehouse about the proposed *Digest.* Lenaugh had heard from *Journal* editors Irving Kahn and Frank Block—both CFAs—that they were decidedly unhappy about the Institute's plans. The substance of their displeasure was twofold. First, there was concern that the ICFA publication would duplicate the "Financial Analysts Digest" feature of the *Journal*; second, there was perhaps even greater concern that the "so-called 'Digest' was to contain original articles stemming from C.F.A. research activities" and thus would compete directly with the main body of the *Financial Analysts Journal,* negating its "long struggle to establish its specialized kind of readers and get out of red ink. . . ."

On March 16, 1966, Dutton Morehouse wrote personally to Frank Block to reassure him of the ICFA's good intentions. "I must admit," Morehouse began, "that I am at considerable loss to understand the idea that the C.F.A. had any intention of creating a competing publication to the *Financial Analysts Journal.*" He continued:

> The background of "The Digest" begins with a discussion one Sunday morning in Charlottesville after the Trustees meeting when we were trying to list all the ideas that anyone could come up with as to programs which might be of interest to C.F.A.'s. Among those ideas was a short digest of articles in various financial journals similar to the publication of the Harvard Business School which I think was called "The Executive." Presumably, articles in the Analysts Journal would also have been digested.

Concerning the *Journal* editors' misapprehension that such a digest would contain original articles, Morehouse stated flatly that this certainly was not so. In fact, he noted, "such material would be printed in the *Journal* if the editors accepted it." Furthermore, although Morehouse did not delineate it, the concern that the proposed digest would compete with the *Journal*'s "Digest" was also based on a misunderstanding: the latter was a digest of news and features of general interest to analysts, while the proposed *CFA Digest* was to consist of abstracted articles from scholarly and professional journals. There was actually no overlap at all.

Although Block and the *Journal* editors may have been reassured by Morehouse's letter, the proposed *CFA Digest* did not come into existence for several years—largely because the Institute had neither the financial nor personnel resources to implement it. By the summer of 1969, however, the ICFA's leaders felt such a publication could be undertaken and proposed its inception to the FAF Policy and Planning Committee that summer. The proposal, which was submitted by Stewart Sheppard and Institute president Barlow, specified that the magazine was intended "primarily for gratuitous distribution to the Institute's membership." Its purpose was to give those members "some tangible return for the annual fees they now pay to keep their C.F.A. designation in good standing."

On September 5, 1969, Barlow wrote to Frank Block, who was by then president of the Financial Analysts Federation, further spelling out the agreed-upon terms of such a publication. To avoid conflict with the *Journal*, Barlow stipulated that the proposed digest should not carry paid advertising or editorial material, and would not—either overtly or covertly—seek paid subscriptions. Edmund Mennis was appointed editor (a capacity in which he served through 1986); the proposed editorial board contained several members of the Institute's Research and Publication Committee, including Frank Block himself. Other board members were William R. Amos, CFA; Charles N. Berents, CFA; M. Harvey Earp, CFA; Andrew P. Ferretti, CFA; Robert B. Johnson, CFA; Marshall D. Ketchum, CFA; Robert T. Morgan, CFA; Jerome L. Valentine, CFA; and Peter F. Way, CFA.

The protocol of approval by the Federation's directors was delayed pending a discussion of the matter by *Digest* editor Ed Mennis, who was an associate editor of the *FAJ*, with the *Journal's* editorial board. At the close of 1969, Frank Block was able to write to Leonard Barlow that "all seems to be well." Yet by the end of Barlow's presidency the following spring, the *Digest* had not been published. This further delay was largely due to personnel insufficiencies at the Institute. Gerald MacFarlane, who had been research assistant since 1967, went to work for the SEC in the late spring of 1970. Moreover, Stewart Sheppard was still dividing his time between New York and Charlottesville. His return in July

1970 at the urging of Ed Mennis, who became ICFA president that summer, enabled the Digest plans to proceed. Sheppard added personnel. Robert H. Trent of the University of Virginia faculty was taken on as Research Administrator, and Mary Shelton as the Digest's circulation manager, while two graduate students were hired as assistants. By fall 1970, this new research staff had begun identifying those journals likely to be sources of abstract material and had started digesting general articles, including "classic articles" on finance no longer readily available.

Although settling questions about taxes, permission forms, abstractors and frequency of publication took several more months, the first issue was ready for distribution to Institute members in July 1971 and was well received. Subsequent issues were available in the fall of 1971 and winter, spring and summer of 1972, establishing the *Digest* on its originally projected quarterly schedule. The intent of the *Digest* was, in Mennis' words, "to bridge partially the gap between the practitioner and the academician." Reactions from readers indicated the *Digest* was filling this need. By the end of its first year of publication, the *CFA Digest* had attracted over two hundred unsolicited paid subscribers and a gratifyingly "favorable response." In May 1972, Mennis was able to report to the ICFA trustees that the "many letters and verbal comments from . . . members" had served to assure the *Digest* editorial board and Institute staffffthat the goal of providing part of a continuing education program for ICFA members through the quarterly *Digest* had been achieved.

*   *   *

In addition to the *CFA Digest,* the ICFA intended to provide other services which would enable Institute members to further their professionalism. Mindful of this, Mennis and the trustees appointed an ad hoc committee on continuing education, chaired by Mary Petrie, in May 1971. In September of that year it was established as a permanent standing committee. Its purpose, according to the Bylaws, was "to formulate and recommend procedures and programs for the continuing improvement of the professional competence of Chartered Financial Analysts." Among the programs most seriously considered were "intensive seminars," either for small groups in Charlottesville or larger ones in New York. The former was favored because large meetings in New York might present "a serious problem of competition with both the Federation and the New York Society."

For several years, however, the Institute would concentrate its continuing education efforts on publications rather than seminars. Early in 1972, Petrie's committee had noted "the proliferation of seminar workshop meetings planned by the Financial Analysts Federation and various Societies" and had "questioned the additional demand for this type of educational activity." Because of the Institute's concern about competing directly with the Federation, and also because of the CFA Research Foundation's continuing series of seminars, the ICFA did not conduct any seminars until the spring of 1974 (and then sponsored them jointly with the Research Foundation). In the interim, the free distribution of the *CFA Digest* and other Institute publications to members comprised the continuing education program.

The ICFA also worked to consolidate its professionalism by providing members with copies of the Institute's Basic Documents, which included the Articles of Incorporation, the Bylaws, the Code of Ethics, Standards of Professional Conduct, and the Rules of Procedure. In addition, in the summer of 1971 the Institute sent a brochure entitled "The Profession of Financial Analysis and the Chartered Financial Analyst" to members and to various corporate and government officials. The brochure was a concise account of the profession in general and of the history and activities of the Institute, written mainly by Robert H. Perry of San Francisco under the auspices of the Public and Industry Relations Committee.

This program of distributing publications to members free of charge was undertaken at considerable cost to the Institute — a cost that was difficult for the Institute to absorb, for its financial resources were severely strained. Mennis recalls that during his terms of office, "finances always were a problem. . . . " In fact, for several years before Mennis's presidency, the Institute had been running in the red, issuing "a dreary series of budgets in deficit" as costs outpaced income. Although the ICFA's financial outlook was improved when the FAF forgave the $40,000 debt owed by the Institute in February 1970, deficits continued. The extent of the problem was masked somewhat because the Institute's accounts were kept on a cash basis; however, after the accounting system was switched to an accrual basis on August 31, 1971, it became very clear that the ICFA's financial problems were serious.

The credit for untangling the Institute's finances goes to Mary Petrie, secretary-treasurer in 1971-72. According to Frank Block, who succeeded Ed Mennis as Institute president in the summer of 1972, "we shall never be able to thank Mary Petrie enough for her analysis of the Institute's budgeting process." The trouble was twofold, relating to projected revenues on the one hand, and dues and fees on the other. Projected revenues had been "based on expectations that everyone who was registered in the program and eligible to take an exam would take it at the earliest possible date," in Frank Block's words. Such expectations were not always realistic. In addition, the number of candidate registrations had begun to decline by the early 1970s. Given the uncertain employment conditions in the industry, the Institute could expect a substantial reduction in enrollments. As Petrie put it, "ICFA trustees were very worried that the number of registrants for the examination program would begin to decline at the very time the organization itself was going with attendant expenses [that] made accurate budgeting difficult.... "

Besides the difficulty in predicting new and continuing registrations, the Institute's finances had been jeopardized by a relatively stagnant fee and dues structure. By 1973, the ICFA had been giving exams and awarding charters for 10 years, but had not increased dues, despite inflationary pressures. As Mennis remembers, "We didn't have that many members and we were most reluctant to increase dues (at least, not until we had done something for the charter holders)." The examination program had seen a fee increase in 1967, but none sufficient to meet all its expenses.

At the board meeting held on September 12, 1971, the trustees decided to raise fees in order to make the examination financially self-sustaining. Not until a year later, however, were members' dues increased, and then only by $10.00. These increases, coupled with cost-cutting measures recommended by Robert Milne's Ways and Means Committee (see Chapter 8), were necessary to save the Institute from serious financial difficulties.

*   *   *

Despite its very real financial woes, the ICFA was in a position of strength at the end of its first decade. Under the leadership of Mennis, Barlow, Watterson, and Sheppard, and thanks to countless hours of committee work, the Institute had realized its goal of enhancing professionalism within the analyst community. However, 1972 was also a year of transition, both literally and figuratively. It was decided to relocate ICFA headquarters from Faulkner House to a less costly location on the western outskirts of Charlottesville. But the Institute was changing in another, more significant way as well. The work of organizing was over, and the task of defining the profession of financial analysis, though essentially never-ending, was complete to the extent that its parameters had been established. Through the Institute's work, financial analysis, as a profession, had "an identified but evolving body of knowledge," a strong examination program to test that knowledge, and an enforceable code of ethics. These would continue to be refined, but by 1972 the ICFA had defined the basic elements of its furtherance of professionalism.

A very crucial change for the Institute occurred in the spring of 1972, when Stewart Sheppard announced his resignation as executive director, effective September 1. On that date, Sheppard would become dean of Virginia's Colgate Darden Graduate School of Business, succeeding his long-time friend and colleague, Charles Abbott. The loss of Stewart Sheppard was difficult to overcome.

Throughout his 11 years of service, Sheppard had personified the progress of the Institute, just as Abe Kulp personified its creation. Kulp had taken Ben Graham's original idea and given it shape; Sheppard had made it work. When Kulp was searching for a director for the ICFA in 1960 and 1961, he noted that the chosen individual must be "adamant on high standards." No one was more so than Sheppard. His extraordinary devotion to enhancing professionalism among analysts, by insisting that the Institute maintain high intellectual and ethical standards, is apparent in everything he wrote pertaining to the CFA program. Sheppard took the idea of professionalizing financial analysis, and with the assistance of Ray Smith (who also left in 1972) and the various trustees and committee members, turned it into a strong, self-sustaining program of examinations, publications, and ethical enforcement that was able to survive the loss of his leadership.

In a report on his own last year as Institute president, Ed Mennis announced Sheppard's departure with "a note of sadness." The Institute was proud of the recognition of Sheppard evidenced by his appointment as Dean, but nonetheless regretful at his departure. Sheppard, Mennis wrote, "leaves with our heartfelt thanks" and "leaves behind him 11 years of dedicated service . . . responsible for the growth of the Institute to a well recognized professional organization in the financial community." Finally, Mennis noted, Sheppard's "wisdom and leadership will be an inspiration to those who will carry forward the task to which he has given so much of himself." The outgoing president—to whom the Institute also owed much thanks—did not exaggerate when he said of Sheppard, "the debt we owe him can never be repaid."

PART FOUR

THE INSTITUTE AS INDUSTRY STANDARD

The CFA Examination program is in itself a most rewarding educational experience for those who take the study materials seriously. There seems little doubt that the exposure to this educational experience has substantially changed the way in which money is invested today. . . .

Frank Block, March 3, 1976

The evolution of new techniques in this field has been rapid. I say that as I look at my own Charter, with the date of 1966 on it, realizing that many aspects of the current body of knowledge on which we test candidates are known to me only in the most general terms.

C. Roderick O'Neil,
15th ICFA President,
to Charles D. Ellis,
20th ICFA President,
August 16, 1978

CHAPTER EIGHT
Regulation or Self-Regulation?

The man chosen to carry forward Stewart Sheppard's work was W. Scott Bauman. Like Sheppard, Bauman had a strong academic background. At the time of his ICFA appointment, Bauman was head of the Department of Finance and Business Economics in the Graduate School of Management and Business at the University of Oregon, having taught finance and investments at the University of Toledo and Indiana University. Educated at Michigan and Indiana, Bauman also had practical experience as an investment analyst at Wells Fargo Bank, and as a securities broker with a New York Stock Exchange member firm. He was known to the analyst community for his various writings on investments and finance. Like his predecessor, Bauman was appointed to the Darden faculty where he was to spend one-third of his time teaching; the remaining two-thirds were devoted to Institute administration.

Unlike Stewart Sheppard, however, Scott Bauman was a CFA, chartered in 1967. In addition, he had served as a grader for several years, and had been a member of Gil Palmer's Council of Examiners since 1970. He was thus intimately familiar with the workings of the examination program at a time when the Institute's primary function was still administering exams. By 1972, however, the ICFA was beginning to work towards a continuing education program. Bauman saw the expansion of this program as one of his main tasks. When he assumed the directorship, he recalls, "the Institute had 1,486 active candidates, but 3,218 members." He felt that the ICFA would need to "develop educational programs for its constituent members if it were to provide ongoing leadership in the continuing development of the profession."

However, Bauman's plans for continuing education had to be put aside temporarily in favor of more pressing issues such as the ICFA's financial problems. Even if a continuing education program was formulated, it could not be implemented, because the Institute's resources were so strained. Institute President Frank Block had appointed an ad hoc committee on Ways and Means, under the direction of trustee Robert D. Milne. At the Board meeting held September 9, 1972, during which Stewart Sheppard passed the position of executive director to Scott Bauman, the trustees discussed areas that Milne's committee might investigate.

The Institute was in the red, as it had been for several years and would "end the year with a deficit of sizeable proportions," stated Frank Block. Cost-cutting measures were needed promptly, as any benefits from the dues increase would not be felt for at least another year. One area in which expense reductions were pursued immediately was the cost of administering the examinations. As of 1972, the ICFA had been giving exams at fifty-seven centers in North America, and six abroad. Milne's committee considered ways to lessen the expense of this widespread administration, reducing the number of centers in large metropolitan areas and perhaps dropping small examination centers altogether. Another potential means of saving money was to make the grading process more efficient by ensuring that graders were available for the full ten days and thus, in Sheppard's opinion, reduce travel costs and "starting-up" time. In addition, President Block suggested that the ICFA trustees grade for no fee.

Another area to be explored as a source of increased revenues was the CFA Research Foundation. From its founding in 1965 through the fall of 1972, the Research Foundation had been receiving certain services free from the Institute. These services were largely in the form of support staff, but also included some research, and assistance in the dissemination of publications. There was a certain logic to this, of course, because the Foundation literature was published for CFAs. However, in the fall of 1972, the Foundation's trustees had begun to see that its mission was broader than originally conceived, and consequently changed the Foundation's title to "The Financial Analysts Research Foundation" (FARF) — in recognition of its function "to conduct both basic and applied research of a disinterested nature . . . which is of potential value not only to the practitioner, but also to regulatory agencies and the academic community." Additionally, in 1971 the Foundation had launched an extensive fundraising campaign, and by September 1972 had collected $73,000 of its $120,000 goal. In view of FARF's improved financial picture and its expanded mission, the Institute's trustees decided to begin billing the Foundation for services that had previously been rendered free. They continued such billing annually.

In January 1973, Robert Milne's Ways and Means Committee presented the Institute trustees with additional recommendations for cutting costs. The number of examination centers was to be decreased, with centers in remote areas to be opened only at a charge to the candidates, and even then only if a sufficient number of candidates would be using them. The committee also recommended that the ICFA Directory decrease its publication to every other year. Although these and other changes were implemented gradually and with a certain reluctance on the part of the trustees, they were effective. As Frank Block put it, "1971-72 had come in with a horrible deficit of almost $33,000, bringing the fund balance to a deficit of $71,000. Yet, by late 1973 we were all breathing a sigh of relief." The reduced costs, coupled with an unexpected increase in candidate enrollments, had helped the Institute show a net income of almost $40,000 for 1972-73, bringing the net worth deficit down to $31,000 — despite the one-time expense of moving to its new location at the Boar's Head office complex. "Of course," as Block noted, "the members [had] gotten practically no services from the Institute that year." But neither had they seen their Institute go under. Instead, it had been put on a sound financial footing that ultimately enabled it to provide more for its members than originally anticipated, thanks to Mary Petrie's budget analysis and to the work of Robert Milne's Ways & Means Committee. But for a while, things had been shaky. Frank Block, who presided over most of the period of cost-cutting and revenue-increasing, summed it up this way: "I felt great my year was over, and we didn't go broke."

*   *   *

Although fiscal problems preoccupied the Institute throughout 1972, by 1973 a compelling new issue emerged: the possibility of a merger between the Institute and the Financial Analysts Federation. In May 1972, Robert T. Morgan, who had just become president of the FAF, met with Frank Block, the incoming ICFA president, to discuss Morgan's belief that a merger of the two organizations would be desirable. Both men could see that certain efficiencies and economies would result from such an action. Block recognized that "there would certainly be many advantages in having a single organization, speaking with a single voice, for professional financial analysts." Such a "single voice" was becoming particularly necessary in the early 1970s, because the SEC was once again growing restive about the investment industry. As Block remembers it:

> The SEC was stirring about, frustrated with concern about the quality of investment advisors. . . . It was clear that [they were] interested in getting into the examination and oversight of investment in a much more vigorous way, and they were open to delegating the activity to an outside body if the right sort could be found.

A single organization of analysts might perform the same type of self-regulatory function that the SEC had delegated to the National Association of Securities Dealers.

Whatever clear benefits might accrue regarding self-regulation, the proposed merger had some disadvantages that gave Block pause. Probably the biggest initial impediment he foresaw, lay in the terms of membership. Block viewed "individual membership in an association as being the central issue, simply because the individual is the unit of self discipline, of professional competence and of submission to the broad needs of society." The Institute, of course, had only individual memberships, attained upon passage of the three exams and maintained by continued adherence to the Code of Ethics and Standards of Professional Conduct. But would individual membership be feasible for the approximately 10,000 Federation members who were not CFAs? The Institute would hardly welcome members who had not met its requirements. The issue of "grandfathering" had delayed the ICFA's creation for years and had been resolved only when it was agreed that no one could gain Institute membership without having passed at least one examination. From the Institute's point of view, a merger would have to be contingent upon some satisfactory resolution of the problem of individual membership through examination versus the Federation policy of membership via a local society.

The immediate result of the Morgan-Block meeting was not a merger arrangement, but rather some generalized thinking about what kind of organization would best serve the diverse needs of the analyst community. To stimulate such thinking, Robert Morgan asked Ed Mennis to prepare "proposals for a professional organization of financial analysts without any consideration given to the then existing organizational structure." Mennis submitted ideas that he regarded as "highly tentative," to stimulate discussion about how to "draw the disparate groups into which analysts are now organized . . . into one cohesive professional body." The emphasis on professionalism was central to Mennis's proposal, as it would be to the ICFA officers and membership. Like Block, Mennis advocated direct membership in any subsequent national organization.

In July 1972, Frank Block met with Robert Morgan, president of the FAF, and with David Watterson, president of the Research Foundation, to discuss Ed Mennis' suggestions for an ideal organization for analysts. In their talks, the three paid "little regard . . . to what exists now or has existed in the past." The meeting resulted in a "Discussion Paper," drafted by Frank Block, and circulated in confidence to the officers of the Institute, Federation, and Foundation. This relative secrecy was necessary because the "Discussion Paper" was potentially controversial, for it paralleled Mennis's proposals for individual membership and centralized organizational structure. From the Institute's point of view, the only plausible way to merge with the FAF (or become part of a new, single, professional analyst organization) was to maintain the purity of the CFA award by having different levels of membership. Anyone wanting full, voting membership would logically have to be or become a Chartered Financial Analyst. Those who had received their charters, particularly the older, established analysts, felt they had put themselves on the line for the betterment of the profession. Anyone wishing to be recognized as a professional analyst ought to do the same.

But the Institute's was not the only point of view. When the ICFA was formed a decade earlier, it created a certain amount of divisiveness within the Federation, but did not overtly affect anyone's standing as a Federation member. One could be a CFA or not; at the outset no one even knew if chartering would last. But the reorganization of the Federation for a merger with the Institute was a clear threat (should direct membership result, as was likely).

Despite the recognized controversies involved, merger talks continued. Many organizational details needed to be worked out: who would be responsible for research, educational programs, publications, ethical enforcement? How large should the administration be, and what would its responsibilities entail, both in terms of a centralized staff and a geographically scattered group of trustees? Block met the Federation's Policy and Planning Committee at Sea Island, Georgia, in December 1972, to discuss some of these specific problems. The meeting resulted in a draft memorandum of reorganization that reflected the Federation's thinking—providing for the "grandfathering" of present members, but admitting new members only providing they became CFAs within ten years.

In January 1973, the Institute's officers held a special joint meeting with their counterparts in the Federation, for which Scott Bauman wrote a tentative reorganization proposal. No formal reorganization was adopted at that meeting; however, the idea of a merger was agreed to in principle. The ICFA trustees, at their own special meeting held later that same month, adopted the following resolution, which was circulated to members via the April 1973 CFA Newsletter:

> RESOLVED THAT in order to enhance the professionalism of financial analysis, it is the sense of the Board that, in principle, a merger of the I.C.F.A. and F.A.F. is desirable, provided that the surviving body will have as its objective a professional organization of financial analysts that will not operate to diminish the significance of the C.F.A. Charter.

The board felt that no action should be taken on a merger, or even on details thereof, until the Institute members had a chance to voice their opinions. Institute vice president Mary Petrie continued to refine the generalized objectives of a merger and the functions of any resulting organization, furthering the work done by Ed Mennis, Frank Block, and Scott Bauman. Yet, everything was held in check until ICFA members could be informed via the April *Newsletter* and respond at the Institute's Annual Meeting, to be held on May 7, 1973, in Washington, D.C. The latter was to be devoted to a "town meeting," to discuss the possible merger. Institute members would also be sent documents from Frank Block and Robert Morgan, outlining their thoughts on the resolution in a general way, agreeing in principle to a merger. Institute members unable to attend were urged to send their comments to Scott Bauman.

The responses ran decidedly against a merger. Though many of those CFAs responding recognized the political desirability of having a single analyst organization, few could see how a merger would do much to enhance, "the continued development of professionalism which is the very heart of the Institute of Chartered Financial Analysts," as one CFA commented. Others feared it would be a "retrograde step" and serve to diminish the significance of the charter. Sentiments at the "town meeting" in May ran similarly high, and as the September *CFA Newsletter* reported, "no official action was taken regarding the suggested merger."

The difficult issue continued to be "purity versus large numbers," as Frank Block had described it nearly a year earlier.

After nearly a decade of striving to refine and enhance professionalism, the Institute had a strong stake in insisting on standards. Thus, Block wrote, "to be a true professional organization," any association resulting from an ICFA/FAF merger must restrict full membership "to those who may reasonably be presumed to be true professionals." The organization must be pure. Yet, to have political and regulatory clout, it must be large. The Federation's 15,000 members were more likely to carry political weight than the Institute's 4,000, and as Block noted, "large numbers have advantages, including political impact in dealing with outsiders, the ability to raise substantial funds for services to members, research, publication, etc." For the time being, however, Institute members were unwilling to sacrifice purity for the power of large numbers.

*   *   *

Given the predictable reluctance of CFA members to dilute their own sense of hard-earned professionalism, why would the Federation's officers—many of them CFAs—pursue the possibility of a merger?

On a philosophical level, many Federation leaders (and some Institute leaders as well) believed that a single organization would best represent the profession. In a Federation memorandum dated December 1972, the FAF leaders expressed it this way:

> To much of the public, including the SEC, and many of our own members as well, the present duality of analyst organization is confusing. . . . We are on the threshold of greater recognition as a profession but we must present a strong, united front. We need unity . . . if we are to respond confidently to the accelerating rate of change in market structure, regulation, standards of professional conduct, corporate reporting and accounting, and investment management performance.

Moreover, to Robert Morgan, the FAF president who first proposed the merger, the time seemed especially favorable, as he remarked in a letter to Ed Mennis in July 1972: "I am very conscious of the tremendous difficulties in attaining the goal . . . [but] the time is right for a truly professional organization and that we may not have a better opportunity if we wait too long a time." What was "right" about the early 1970s was that the Federation leaders were composed primarily of CFAs, and had been for several years. Any proposed merger would not face opposition from Federation leadership.

On a more mundane level, the FAF was facing some internal difficulties that a merger might help to resolve. Like the Institute, the Federation was experiencing severe financial strain in the early 1970s. Unlike the ICFA, however, the FAF could not as readily increase revenues, given the Federation's constituency: societies, not individuals. In fact, when a dues increase was proposed in the spring of 1973, the Federation's largest constituency, the New York Society of Security Analysts, balked, voting "no" on the increase and instead proposed a restructuring of the FAF to better reflect the NYSSA's numbers. In 1973, the NYSSA comprised over a third of the Federation's members, but had delegate strength of under 3 percent, although its members typically comprised about 30 percent of the Board of Directors. At its beginnings, the Federation's founders (who included Lucien Hooper, George Hansen, and Dutton Morehouse) had worked to compensate for New York's natural strength of numbers in order to promote a feeling of unity among the member societies. Some 25 years later, however, the NYSSA's leadership was finding this arrangement intolerable.

The New York Society's proposals did not carry the day in 1973; nor did its dissatisfactions diminish, notwithstanding that at the fall 1973 conference the governing structure was amended, entitling the NYSSA to about 25 percent of the delegates votes and three directors-at-large. An NYSSA "rebellion" surfaced again between 1973 and 1976, fueled by the one issue that served to keep ICFA/FAF merger proposals alive more than any other. The issue was regulation.

Although self-regulation—that is, regulation by one's peers—is always a difficult proposition, it was particularly troublesome for the Federation, since policing rested upon the individual societies.

Individual and local loyalties made it difficult for analysts to apply discipline within local societies. The ICFA, however, which was an organization with direct membership throughout the United States and Canada, did not face the same problems. Ethical enforcement was still problematic, but the removal of responsibility to the regional and national—rather than local—level insured an enhanced ability to act for the betterment of the profession without the influence of personal loyalties or collegial concerns.

Furthermore, the Institute had been strengthening its enforcement abilities consistently since the late 1960s. The work of the Professional Ethics Committee in the years 1968 through 1972 (see Chapter 6) saw a refinement of the ICFA's Code of Ethics and Standards of Professional Conduct. In 1970, the Professional Grievances Committee (now called the Professional Conduct Committee) was formed, and its ability to function was augmented in 1971 by the establishment of 10 regional subcommittees. By the time Scott Bauman joined the Institute as executive director in 1972, several ethics cases were under investigation. Bauman found that the "existing procedures for investigating and imposing sanctions were extremely cumbersome," and worked with legal counsel John Gillis to redraft them throughout 1973. Among the significant changes made and approved by the trustees in September 1973 was to allow the executive director to "enter into an agreed sanction with a member, called a stipulation . . . " as well as to "suspend the charter of a member who fails to respond to reasonable requests from the Institute for factual information" in Scott Bauman's words. Accused charterholders could not simply ignore the Institute's investigations.

As a result of the changes and the intensified level of investigative work, the Institute stipulated its first disciplinary sanctions on April 28, 1974: two charters were revoked, one public censure and a year's suspension imposed, and two private admonishments rendered. It was "the first time that a national professional organization of financial analysts imposed sanctions on its members . . . [and] was evidence that the Institute was not only able but willing to enforce high standards of conduct on its membership," Bauman recalls proudly.

The imposition of sanctions could not have come at a more propitious time. In the early 1970s, the SEC had been manifesting a growing uneasiness about the possible incompetence of investment advisers, for whom uniform standards of qualification did not exist. The early 1970s were a time, as one CFA put it, "of violently fluctuating security market prices, increasing losses in investor portfolios, and a greater likelihood of customer reaction to professional advisors. . . . " Complaints to regulatory bodies abounded in such a climate. In light of this, the Commission had issued a report on the investment management services available to individual investors. In addition, Commissioner Hugh Owens had given a speech on investment adviser regulation that was reprinted in the *Financial Analysts Journal* (January/February 1973). Clearly, the SEC was taking an active interest in the regulation problem.

During this period, the Federation was actively studying the matter of professional qualifications through its Qualifications Committee (established in January 1973 and chaired by Walter P. Stern, later an Institute president), and with several Institute representatives. In December 1973, the committee proposed the Federation Private Self-Regulation Program based on individual Federation membership and with exclusive power to set professional standards and to impose disciplinary sanctions.

At the same time, the New York Society of Security Analysts, which represented over a third of the Federation's membership, was considering the possibility of state licensing of analysts. The Society had drafted a bill, for submission to its state legislature early in 1974, to establish the designation "Certified Security Analyst (CSA)" in New York State. The bulk of NYSSA members would be "grandfathered in" upon the enactment of this legislation; new members would have to meet age, experience, educational, and character requirements and to pass either the NYSE examination for supervisory analysts or the CFA Level I exam. Regulation of "CSAs" would fall to the NYSSA's Ethics Committee and that of the Rochester Society, which in effect would jointly become an arm of the New York State Attorney

General's office. On February 6, 1974, this bill to license and regulate analysts was introduced into the New York state legislature.

Although it was theoretically a local society matter, the proposed New York State legislation had potentially great ramifications for all analysts. Given the size of the NYSSA membership and the interstate nature of the financial industry, many—if not most—analysts did business in New York. In addition, the Institute was not happy with several components of the NYSSA plan, beyond the obvious potential for confusion in the public's mind between CSAs and CFAs. Particularly unsatisfactory was the blanket "grandfathering" of current society members. The Institute's founders had fought too long against such a system for its present officers to look favorably upon this. The possible substitution of the NYSE's examination for the Institute's Level I examination as sufficient evidence of qualification was also objectionable; ICFA leaders did not think them comparable.

When it became clear that the NYSSA bill was to be filed, the Federation—with the cooperation and support of the Institute—commenced extensive communications with its member societies, individual members, industry and firm leaders, regulators and legislators. During January and February, Federation chairman Eugene H. Vaughan (later an Institute trustee), wrote the Federation membership and delegates and visited numberous societies advocating the FAF private program rather than state regulation, explaining the merits and advantages of each approach. These efforts, coupled with those of the Institute, likely represented the most intensive communications with the membership and financial community ever carried out by these organizations.

Before the legislation was even introduced, Mary Petrie, who succeeded Frank Block as ICFA president in May 1973, requested that Scott Bauman meet with David Clurman, assistant attorney general of New York, to explain the Institute's position "that it would be preferable for financial analysts to be regulated by their own professional organization rather than by the government...." Bauman also indicated that any regulation—whether self-imposed or governmental—should be at the national level, because of the profession's interstate nature. Bauman also joined in a conference with Clurman and Federation and NYSSA representatives at which opposition to the legislation was presented by both the Institute and Federation.

Petrie and Bauman were quick to inform the Institute membership of the NYSSA's actions. In the December 1973 *CFA Newsletter*, they outlined the proposal and, while acknowledging that the Society was acting "out of concern" over the possibility of Federal regulation, voiced the Institute's objections to what the NYSSA was recommending. In addition, Petrie communicated directly with the Institute's members in January 1974, informing them of the Federation's position on "developing a strong national self-regulatory structure" and of the ICFA trustees' unqualified opposition to "certain provisions" of the New York bill. She also urged them to convey "to the Federation, the New York Society, and to the Attorney General," as well as the Institute, any comments or suggestions they might have. Petrie likewise wrote to New York Attorney General Louis Lefkowitz, expressing the ICFA's position. The following month, Bauman sent a letter to all New York CFAs, urging them to "study this issue and make your views known immediately" to state, society, and federation officials.

During February, after both the Federation self-regulation and state regulation proposals had been revealed to the membership, a Federation poll of members outside New York opposed the NYSSA bill by ten to one, and a NYSSA poll of its members opposed the bill by a two to one margin. Subsequently, the FAF delegates adopted its Private Self-Regulation Plan on April 28, 1974, and within two years the individual members of all societies were included in it.

The views of the New York CFAs, the Institute, and the Federation were apparently heeded, for the legislation was deferred. Proposals for some form of licensing and state entitlement as CSAs (later changed to PSA, or "Professional Security Analyst") continued to have considerable life within the New York Society, however. A revised state licensing bill sponsored by the NYSSA was introduced in February 1976, and again vigorously opposed by the Federation and Institute. Not until May 1976, when a slate of officers opposing those who had propounded the idea of state licensing was elected, were such proposals withdrawn. This election marked the resolution of what Institute president Walter Stern called "the internecine warfare between the New York Society of Security Analysts and the rest of the Federation" and resulted in bringing "the whole profession under one disciplinary and ethics umbrella."

The withdrawal of the New York State licensing proposals did not signal the end of concern over governmental regulation, however. By the mid-1970s, Congress was considering amendments to the Investment Advisers Act of 1940, to authorize the SEC to "prescribe standards of qualification and financial responsibility" for such advisers. Given the Institute's "unmitigated desire to self-regulate"—as Carl Beckers had put it—such governmentally prescribed standards were unwelcome. In the hopes of warding them off, Scott Bauman and Institute presidents Robert E. Blixt (1975-76) and Walter P. Stern (1976-77) testified before Senate and House subcommittees in Washington in February and May 1976. Their statements emphasized the professional nature of the Institute: the regulatory and qualifying institution prescribed by the proposed amendments already existed. The Institute of Chartered Financial Analysts *was* that institution.

The professionalization that the ICFA officers stressed was, they believed, most visible in two areas: the examination program and the enforcement of ethical standards. Bauman cited statistics on the increase in candidates over the Institute's 13 year history, the passing and failing rates on various exams, and the percentage of FAF members earning ICFA membership—a figure that had grown from 3 percent at the program's outset to over 30 percent in 1975 (and over 40 percent if active candidates were included). Perhaps even more germane to the goals of those interested in amending the Investment Advisers Act of 1940 was the Institute's effective enforcement of ethical standards.

In his February 1976 testimony, Bauman presented a report prepared by Michael P. Dooley, a University of Virginia law professor, formerly of the New York law firm Dewey, Ballantine, who had become the Institute's Special Counsel in 1974. Dooley's report detailed for the Senate subcommittee the Institute's ethical standards as well as its procedures for identifying and investigating alleged violations. Dooley also listed the 10 cases "in which definitive affirmative action has been taken to date." Institute members had been investigated for misuse of confidential information, for failure to supervise properly, for conflict of interest, for sale of unregistered securities, misrepresentation, and outright securities fraud. In 6 of the 10 cases, Dooley noted, "investigations were commenced on the basis of the member's response to the Ethical Conduct Questionnaire" that charterholders filled out annually. Out of the remaining 4 cases initiated, 3 cases were by other Institute members; and 1 by a member's client. Of the total 10 cases, 3 were undertaken by the Institute subsequent to SEC or NASD actions; 4 after consent orders from outside regulatory agencies; 1 after a member's indictment; and 2 when "there had been no action taken by any governmental or regulatory agency."

Noting that these cases had resulted in 3 charter revocations, 2 public censures, 1 suspension, 3 private admonishments, and 1 dismissal of charges by the ICFA trustees, Dooley's report informed the Senate subcommittee of the Institute's growing effectiveness as a self-regulatory body. The year 1975 alone had seen 23 cases of possible violations under investigation by the Institute's executive director and, where appropriate, by a hearing panel of one of the Professional Grievance Regional Subcommittees. Moreover, as Dooley noted, "an increasing number of cases are being developed independently of governmental or regulatory agency action."

The ability of the Institute to act independently in investigating possible violations by its members was of considerable significance. Though circumstances often might dictate that the Institute's enforcement procedures follow the actions of governmental agencies, those testifying before the House and Senate Subcommittees, and those involved with the ICFA enforcement process in general, wanted to ensure that the Institute's ability to function as an independent investigative force be understood.

M. Harvey Earp, who guided the Professional Conduct Committee during its early years of activity, was particularly determined to establish the primacy of the committee's investigations and their independence. As he remarked in a letter to Scott Bauman later in 1976, "It is the Professional Conduct Committee's strong opinion that actions against our members by other regulatory bodies *should not be given primary consideration* in our deliberations *except for the most serious instances.*" It was proper, Earp maintained, "to use the public records as *sources of evidence,* but not *conclusions.* Otherwise, we are de facto delegating our responsibilities to our members to others outside our own professional bodies, and taking from our members the opportunity to be heard independently by their peers."

This process of peer review was a precious right, not to be surrendered lightly to "a group of laymen who might not be knowledgeable of the subtleties of our business, and its professional conduct and ethics," even though peers might judge one more harshly than outside regulatory agencies. Moreover, as Earp noted in the same letter, despite the inevitable expenses involved in carrying out independent investigations, members of the Institute's regional conduct committees were uniquely qualified to complete such work. "After all," he wrote, "we are trained as analysts to be investigators." Such abilities made the Institute's lack of subpoena power less significant. As Earp put it, "let's remember that good newspaper reporters have accomplished more in many cases [than] legally constituted bodies."

Whether acting subsequent to regulatory agencies or proceeding to investigate previously unconsidered violations, Earp's "good reporters" and the Institute's executive director had looked into 111 cases of possible unethical conduct by the end of the 1970s. Over 100 of these complaints had been reported by members on their annual questionnaires. Most had been dismissed without sanction, but in 15 cases ICFA members had been publicly or privately censured or had their charters revoked. The Institute's efforts to maintain a credible program of policing its members did not go unheeded: the proposed legislation to amend the Investment Advisers Act of 1940 did not pass. Nor did an SEC proposal to set qualifying exam requirements for broker-dealer research personnel, which was debated in 1977 and 1978. In both cases, the merits of the ICFA's self-regulatory program seemed to deflect interest in governmental regulation.

The person who was perhaps most responsible for the success of the ICFA's effort to forestall governmental regulation was Scott Bauman. Interest in regulatory activity was high during the years he served as the Institute's executive director. Complemented by work of lawyers John Gillis and Michael Dooley, Bauman's was a tireless effort to maintain and improve the Institute's ability to self-regulate. When Bauman decided to return full time to research and teaching in 1978, after six years as the ICFA director, those who had worked closely with him were quick to acknowledge his achievement. John Gillis congratulated him on his "significant contribution to establishing the viability and credibility of the professional conduct program," while Philip "Pres" Brooks, whose presidency coincided with Bauman's last year, credited him with "diffusing the SEC threat and converting them from an adversary into an ally." Robert Milne, who worked with Bauman in many capacities during their respective tenures at the Institute, expressed the Institute's gratitude strongly:

[Y]our greatest contribution to the profession will go down in history as the development of an active and successful program of self-regulation. This effort was an outstanding evidence of your skills. . . . You had nothing to build upon and created a functioning self-regulation program at a time when many others tackled the problem but did not have the courage and tenacity to attack it properly.

Thanks to Bauman's perseverance, both as champion of the Institute's enforcement program and as its initial investigator, and to the likewise untiring efforts of Harvey Earp in organizing the Professional Conduct Regional Subcommittees and putting their investigative skills to work, the ICFA could indeed convince the investing public at large and the regulatory commissions in particular—that it had a program of ethical enforcement and self-regulation in place that was unmatched in the industry.

*   *   *

Institutional trustees, administrators, and committee workers can easily became caught up in the routine of organizational details. Not often do they have a chance to raise their eyes above the level of papers piled on their desks. Certainly the middle and late 1970s, which saw the Institute staff and officers preoccupied with merger proposals and regulatory matters, afforded few opportunities to step back and look at how far the Institute had come. But in the spring of 1976, five years into its second decade, the Institute of Chartered Financial Analysts was presented with a chance to recognize its achievement by honoring those responsible.

By May 1976, the ICFA was in a position to regard itself as the standard of professionalism in the financial community. The Institute had established a credible program of self-regulation and had an examination program recognized by outside groups as a kind of standard. Not only were the New York Stock Exchange and the Investment Counsel Association of America willing to accept the CFA examinations as evidence of necessary and sufficient professional status, but its own parent organization, the Financial Analysts Federation, had established a fellows program on July 1, 1976, that required of applicants the successful completion of the CFA Level I examination. The Federation members whose dedication to professionalization had led them to establish the Institute had not known whether chartering would survive. In fact, it had thrived, to the point where the Federation had formally sanctioned CFA I as a requirement for membership.

The common purposes of the Institute and the Federation were evident in the next few years as several activities in the area of professional standards become joint endeavors. The Professional Conduct Committees of the two organizations became a joint committee, and the staffs and counsel together developed procedures to coordinate and cooperate in processing matters involving the conduct of the joint members. The Institute's Professional Ethics Committee and the Federaton's Investment

Analysis Standards Board, both charged with responsibility for their organizations' Code of Ethics and Standards of Professional Conduct, also became a joint committee. (The Codes and Standards have been identical since adoption in the 1960s.) This joint committee prepared the *Standards of Practice Handbook*, first published by the Institute and Federation in 1982, which has been applauded by the membership, the investment community, and regulators as an outstanding work in the field of private self-regulation.

Thus, the mid-1970s were an auspicious time for taking pride in the Institute's position. Though the round of small decisions continued—should Montreal test-takers be permitted to write in French and how would the mechanics of translation be handled? should candidates be allowed to use the newly available pocket calculators? what if exams got lost in the mail?—the Board of Trustees, under the direction of Leonard Barlow's Awards Committee, made one big decision that recognized the Institute's whole achievement. It established the C. Stewart Sheppard Award.

The award was intended to acknowledge and honor those members of the Institute who, through dedicated effort and leadership, "rendered outstanding service" to advance the ICFA "as a vital force in fostering the education of financial analysts, establishing high ethical standards of conduct, and developing programs and publications to encourage the continuing education of financial analysts." No one represented these qualities better than Stewart Sheppard himself, whose years of dedication to the CFA program had taken it from an idea to a reality, but the four men who joined Sheppard as the initial recipients of the award that honored him also represented them well: Abe Kulp, George Hansen, Dutton Morehouse, and David Watterson. Among them, the five embodied a commitment to professionalism, knowledge, ethics, and research that more than anything else had helped to bring the Institute to its position of excellence. When they received the award from retiring Institute president Robert Blixt, these five men were to be congratulated on founding and organizing an Institute that had become what they had hoped: the standard of professionalism in the analyst community.

CHAPTER NINE
Upgrading the Examination Program

Although the Institute's attention was turned for several years towards establishing a sound program of self-regulation, its *raison d'etre* remained the examination program. In summarizing the activities of his year as ICFA president, Walter Stern had noted that "we rise and fall in the success of this program." Thus, during the year he served (1976-77), Stern had made a conscious effort "to *reorient priorities* to the *CFA Candidate Program. . . .* " In fact, in the years following Stern's presidency the examination program would receive considerable attention and revamping.

Even prior to this concentrated attention, the exam and study guide cycle had been subject to many refinements. In 1973-74, the General Topic Outline which expressed the profession's body of knowledge underwent its first extensive revision. Institute president Mary Petrie commissioned John Neff, chairman of the Research and Publications Committee at that time, to work together with Ed Mennis, Scott Bauman, and Robert Trent on "the problem of reviewing and revaluing the topical outline" to determine what should be added to it and what should be reorganized. The revised outline, largely Mennis's work, with modifications added by Bauman and Trent, saw the five topic areas of the 1969 version expanded to seven. Quantitative techniques became a separate topic, tested progressively on all three exams, while the techniques of analysis were subdivided into two topic areas, with fixed income and equity securities now tested as discrete topics. All of the study guides were subsequently revised to match the new curriculum under the direction of Hartman "Hap" Butler, an experienced practitioner who joined the staff as education director in 1975.

By the mid-1970s, the CFA Candidate Program had come to be recognized as the standard of professionalism in the industry. The New York Society of Security Analysts, even during its period of estrangement from the FAF, would have accepted successful passage of CFA I for its new members under its proposed licensing plan. The Institute had balked at this, not because it felt CFA I insufficient, but because the NYSSA had also proposed that the New York Stock Exchange's exam for supervisory analysts could be substituted for CFA I. Institute officers and staff, as noted earlier, did not feel the exams were equivalent.

Neither did the NYSE. In 1974, representatives of the New York Stock Exchange had approached the Institute staff regarding cooperation between the two bodies on the preparation of an NYSE Supervisory Analyst examination. Scott Bauman and Examinations Administrator O. Whitfield Broome, a CPA and Virginia faculty member who joined the Institute staff in 1973, met with the NYSE staff; the latter indicated an interest in sanctioning certain of the CFA exams (probably CFA I and II) as sufficient for the designation NYSE Supervisory Analyst. This presented problems for the Institute, as NYSE's exams were given "on demand"—often on a monthly basis—while the Institute's were annual one-day events. The likelihood of the Institute generating monthly exams was not great, given the volunteer nature of the Council of Examiners and the fact that both Broome and Bauman were there only part time. Though the Board of Trustees voted in September 1974 to cooperate with the NYSE in this matter, the Institute did not write separate exams for Supervisory Analysts. Instead, the New York Stock Exchange came to accept the earning of a CFA and, later, the passage of CFA I, as an adequate substitute for their own Supervisory Analyst exam.

The ICFA, thus, was seeing its examination program recognized beyond its own membership. This was particularly true in the case of the Investment Counsel Association of America (ICAA), which for over a decade had been showing interest in some form of affiliation with the CFA program. As early as 1962 the ICAA had approached Stewart Sheppard and Abe Kulp about a potential liaison. In fact, around the same time that Sheppard wryly announced that the warden of Sing Sing was interested in having the Institute help rehabilitate wayward financiers, he also revealed to the trustees the ICAA's interest in having the Institute help write an exam for its members. Because of the exigencies of getting the Institute's fledgling examination program organized and functioning, however, Sheppard and his staff were unable to devote time to the ICAA's needs, and the potential liaison was stalled.

But 11 years later the interest was still there. By 1974 the ICAA had evolved its own species of chartering. Based on a point system, Association members could earn the designation "C.I.C."—Chartered Investment Counselor—by certifying particular experience and education requirements. But the ICAA, whose interests and membership often overlapped the Institute's, wanted a higher degree of professionalism associated with the C.I.C. designation, and looked to the ICFA as the industry standard. Moreover, several prominent Institute members and past presidents—including David Watterson, Robert Milne, Peter Avenali, Jay Vawter, Solon Patterson and Robert H. Perry—belonged to the ICAA, so mutual respect already existed.

In January 1974, Stewart Sheppard, who remained on the Institute Board as an ex officio trustee and had long been interested in an ICFA/ICAA affiliation, approached Scott Bauman and Mary Petrie with a proposal that the Institute undertake "the sponsorship of the C.I.C designation awarded by the Investment Counsel Association of America." The program would be underwritten by the ICAA. For its part, the Institute would construct an "adapted" version of CFA III that would contain some material from levels I and II and some additional material on taxation, estate planning and pension planning. Gilbert Palmer, chairman of the Council of Examiners, would be empowered to expand subcommittee III of the council to accommodate these new questions.

Jay Vawter, later the Institute's 21st president (1984-85), served as the liaison member for the two groups. He and James F. O'Neil, a CFA and business associate of Institute president Robert Milne, were to form the ICAA Subcommittee of Palmer's Council of Examiners. Grandfathering would be minimal and ethical enforcement left to the ICAA, which had a compatible, though different, ethical code. The Institute would prepare and distribute the appropriate study materials. David Croll, a UVa faculty member, was hired to administer the program.

By June 1975, the C.I.C. program was ready to give a "pilot" exam to 11 candidates, among them members of the ICAA's Board of Governors. The C.I.C. test was administered along with that year's CFA exams and graded by Jay Vawter. Like the CFA exams, this pilot C.I.C. exam was subject to a trustee review—via the ICAA's governors. By 1976, the program was fully operational, complete with separate study guides, Council of Examiners members, and graders. The ICFA continued to administer this related program through June 1982. By that time, the pool of available C.I.C. candidates had dwindled considerably. Moreover, the content of the CFA III examination had itself been modified to include areas formerly limited to the C.I.C test—taxation, ERISA, estate planning—as the Council of Examiners grew to realize the importance of such C.I.C. topics to the CFA program. Consequently, the ICAA Board of Governors voted to discontinue the administration of a separate C.I.C.-originated exam in 1983. The designation C.I.C. would instead be awarded to those constituents in member firms who had sufficient experience and who had obtained their CFAs.

*   *   *

The year 1975 marked a transition in the examination program; the Council of Examiners, who wrote the exams, were faced with the resignation of Gilbert H. Palmer. Palmer had been on the Council of Examiners since 1965 and chaired it since 1969. Long-time council member Dick Lambourne remembers Palmer's insistence that council members serve as graders, in order to see how questions were interpreted and answered by actual candidates. As Jay Vawter recalled, Palmer had "done an excellent job and was highly regarded." Throughout his tenure, Palmer emphasized that CFA exam questions should be practical. His work on the council was invaluable, but after 10 years he was tiring of it and asked to be relieved of his duties. The Institute showed its appreciation for Palmer's work by presenting him with the second C. Stewart Sheppard Award in 1977. In citing him for this honor, Institute president Walter Stern wrote, "your work on the Council of Examiners has been truly heroic . . . one of the . . . unheralded jobs in the industry."

Palmer was succeeded as council chairman by Brierly W. Anderson, whose father Corliss Anderson had helped write the first CFA exam. Anderson brought a meticulous attention to detail to his work as chairman and also a strong conviction that the council and the Research and Publications Committee should work cooperatively, as President Stern had been stressing. This coordination was effected in 1977, when the council and the Research and Publications Committee (chaired by William Cornish) began holding joint annual meetings. Under Anderson, the council also continued to identify areas in which readings were lacking, for remedy by the Research and Publications Committee.

Although the *CFA Readings in Financial Analysis* had gone into a large third edition in 1975, the Council of Examiners felt the topics of pension fund and general portfolio management needed additional material. While it would take several years to fill, some progress was made in the gaps in the area of portfolio management through Study Guide reviews and revisions done by the Research and Publications Committee. Coordinated by Hap Butler, who became the Institute's operations director in 1977, the Study Guide revisions were paralleled and supplemented by two subsequent reworkings of *CFA Readings in Financial Analysis*: a fourth edition in 1977 and a fifth in 1981, which, for the first time, contained digests of "classic" articles on finance.

In 1978, Jay Vawter took over the chairmanship of the Council of Examiners from Brierly Anderson, who went on to serve on the Investment Analysts Standards Board/Professional Ethics Committee that jointly coordinated the ethical standards for the Federation and Institute. Vawter, the original liaison from the

Investment Counsel Association of America, had been active on the council for three years. His initial desire was to shift the council's focus to "broad, philosophical issues." A major goal, in his view, was to "reaffirm the importance of the Institute's examination program as an educational experience, as well as a certification of professional knowledge." To ensure this, Vawter's council proposed to structure the examination process "in a more progressive fashion," moving from a "more academic level at Examination I to the more practical approach at Level III," hoping thus "to improve continuity."

For many years the Council of Examiners had been organized by examination level. The three subcommittees would write all the questions in every subject area for CFA I, II, and III, respectively. Towards the end of Vawter's term as council chairman, however, the Examiners were reorganized by topic. Subcommittees now met to write questions on ethics, or accounting, or any of the seven topic areas, and write them for all three levels. Once the questions (and sample answers) were completed, the subcommittees would reform by examination level to finalize the respective exams. As Vawter noted, this topical organization "helped with [the] progressive and continuous nature of exam question development." By providing a sense of continuity in the subject matter at each successive exam level, Vawter and the council hoped to encourage candidates to rely on their judgment and experience, not merely on factual knowledge.

*   *   *

Vawter's tenure as council chairman (1978-82) coincided with an intense surge of knowledge in the profession of financial analysis which continues to this day. As William Cornish had pointed out in a report to Institute members at the end of his year as president (1979-80), it was doubtful that a "Rip Van Winkle, C.F.A., of the Class of 1963, could awaken and pass any examination in 1980." Cornish's predecessor as ICFA president had reached a similar conclusion. C. Roderick O'Neil, who served as president in 1978-79, had likewise warned Institute members that "fewer and fewer existing charter holders, myself included, would be able to pass the more recent exams." Moreover, as O'Neil noted, "this phenomenon takes place at the same time as criticism of the exams themselves for not moving rapidly enough to keep up to date with developments as they occur."

The necessity for charterholders to keep up would eventually evolve into a formal Institute program of continuing education and accreditation. However, the initial burden of incorporating new material on the proliferation of investment vehicles and strategies into the ICFA program fell to the Examiners and the Research and Publications Committee. Knowledge of such previously exotic investments as futures, options, foreign securities and real estate had to be reckoned with, as did taxation and the increasingly sophisticated use of quantitative techniques. A second edition of the Valentine and Mennis *Quantitative Techniques* book in 1979 helped with the latter, while the newer investment instruments were incorporated into the exam and Study Guide sequence in the early 1980s. The challenge facing the Examiners was, as President Cornish put it, to keep "the testing program pertinent," and in doing so, "to stay abreast of change in investment techniques, investment vehicles, and investment needs, and to properly differentiate between that which has value and that which represents a fad. . . . " Thus, through the coordinated efforts of the Research and Publication Committee and the Council of Examiners the 1980 study program saw four new texts introduced and two dozen articles changed. That year, Cornish noted, "Portfolio Management and Economics were thoroughly revised and the Fixed Income Securities area considerably strengthened."

The efforts to update the curriculum, begun in 1979-80, had a lasting impact on the Institute's examination and education programs. Since it first defined the CFA Body of Knowledge in 1969, the Research and Publications Committee had been subdivided by topic area: economics, ethics, financial accounting, fixed income securities, equity securities, portfolio management, and quantitative techniques. Each subcommittee reviewed the existing literature annually to find suitable study material and identify gaps, with an aim of generating new literature where needed—often through the Financial Analysts Research

Foundation. One consistently troublesome area was portfolio management. To rectify some of the problems this topic had been giving the Institute's study program, early in 1979 the trustees commissioned William Cornish, then ICFA vice president, to form a task force to "determine what portfolio management consists of including its scope and the skills needed to be a practitioner thereof" and to find—or supply—appropriate study materials. This task force, called the Portfolio Management Review Committee, consisted of John Maginn, who served as its chairman, William S. Gray, Robert Morrison, Harold Schwind, Donald Tuttle, Jay Vawter and James Vertin. Given the complexity of the project, it was assumed by Cornish and the subcommittee members, the Committee would function for several years.

The seven subcommittee members represented divergent— sometimes clashing—viewpoints on portfolio management, intentionally reflecting the frequent discord within the profession on this topic. Certainly, portfolio management study materials had long posed problems for the industry and the Institute. As far back as the first preparation of a General Topic Outline in 1968-69, the Portfolio Management Subcommittee had been lamenting the lack of material in this field. In the late 1960s, as mentioned earlier, the Institute commissioned the Research Foundation to hold a series of seminars on various aspects of portfolio management. Four seminars and four books resulted, which helped to partially fill the gap. The last seminar, however, had been held in 1970; what was useful in 1970 was not necessarily relevant at the end of the decade.

During 1979, the Portfolio Management Review Subcommittee met four times. Despite the broad spectrum of thought they represented, the seven members managed to maintain "an open and non-contentious environment so that the facts could be separated from the fads . . . so prevalent in the investment business." In fact, according to subcommittee member Jay Vawter, this diverse group developed such "an amazing rapport and camaraderie" that the experience of working on the portfolio management review has become a highlight of the professional careers of those involved. Certainly their work was compelling.

In their first year, the subcommittee drafted a definition of portfolio management and redrafted the relevant "tree of knowledge" found in the Institute's General Topic Outline. The group also conducted a panel discussion on the topic in New Orleans, and engaged Donald E. Fischer of the University of Connecticut, a long standing member of the Council of Examiners, to search out the existing literature in the field. By the middle of 1980, Fischer's literature search had been completed, the major voids identified, and a final topic outline developed. The subcommittee was then faced with the difficult task of filling the gaps, particularly regarding the formulation of policies, maintaining portfolios and responding to changes, and taking into account "socio-politico-economic expectations," as Chairman John Maginn informed the committee.

Throughout the latter half of 1980 the subcommittee considered how to best fill the voids in the literature. Because the committee members believed portfolio management must be reviewed as an ongoing "process," they were particularly determined to feature—and if necessary create—literature that stressed this. The first result of their efforts was the *CFA Readings in Portfolio Management*, published late in 1980. This volume brought together what the committee members considered "the most applicable articles currently available in journals and periodical literature." Besides concentrating the available and pertinent literature in this volume, the committee also decided to generate articles, an approach advocated by member Jim Vertin, the Institute's incoming president in 1981. The result of their work was *Determinants of Investment Portfolio Policy*, published in 1981, which was comprised of articles by committee members Vawter, Tuttle, Maginn, and Gray. Having found a "glaring deficiency" in both study materials and candidate performance in "the whole area of identification and specification of objectives, constraints and the determination of portfolio policies," the authors addressed these specific topics.

Despite the significant contribution made to portfolio management literature by these two volumes, the subcommittee, which by 1981 consisted of six members (Harold Schwind having taken a leave due to business demands) had decided that an even more extensive publication was needed. In March 1981, the committee proposed to the trustees a book-length project, to be edited by Don Tuttle and John Maginn, which would "comprehensively" describe dynamic portfolio management as a decision-making process. The project's intent, its editors wrote, was to integrate "experience, empirical data, hypothesis testing, and most importantly, application in the competitive environment of the real world." The most comprehensive and successful book project undertaken by the Institute, *Managing Investment Portfolios: A Dynamic Process* was published early in 1983, and updated in 1985. Notably, it was written almost entirely by practitioners, most of them CFAs. Its publication marked the culmination of the Institute's concerted attention to one topic through the work of its Portfolio Management Review Committee. The untold hours of work—largely voluntary—that the book represents typified the commitment of CFAs to the betterment of their profession.

The success of the Maginn and Tuttle volume, which has proven as valuable to investment professionals and individual investors as it has to CFA candidates, has sparked the formation of further review subcommittees. To date such reviews have been undertaken on the topics of fixed income analysis (the results of which have been incorporated in the Maginn and Tuttle 1985-86 update of *Managing Investment Portfolios*), economics, and equity securities analysis. The latter subcommittee, chaired by Alfred C. "Pete" Morley, the Institute's seventeenth president and its current chief executive officer, was organized along the same lines as that for portfolio management, and has defined the topic and revised its tree of knowledge for the ICFA's General Topical Outline. In addition, the Institute has sponsored the publication of a new work on the quantitative aspects of analysis. Edited by Mark Kritzman and Stephen Brown, *Quantitative Analysis for Financial Analysts* was published in January 1987. Such subject reviews, as Jay Vawter has envisioned, may produce "a whole library of outstanding literature on the investment decision making process"—all generated by the Institute's scrupulous attention to its examination and study programs.

*   *   *

The changes in curriculum brought about by the review subcommittees were rivaled by changes in the candidates themselves. New candidates' academic preparation emphasized quantifying, portfolio theories, and computer applications more than that of earlier registrants. In addition, the number of candidates was undeniably greater. After the unexpected success of the CFA program in its early years, attracting over 2,000 candidates in 1966, the enrollment levels dropped for several years and then began a steady but unspectacular increase throughout the 1970s. Though no single year of that decade showed a remarkable increase, the continual growth in candidates stretched the Institute's resources in giving and grading examinations. When Scott Bauman became executive director in 1972, for example, the Institute had just administered tests to 1,486 candidates. By the time Bauman left to return to teaching in 1978, the ICFA was once again testing over 2,000. Of course, the 1970s had been "quite hectic in both equity and fixed-income markets," in the words of Pete Morley. This difficult decade for the financial industry was even further complicated by the Securities Act Amendments of 1975, which ushered in negotiated rates and fiercer competition. By the late 1970s, however, those who were going to survive had surfaced, and the Institute had a wider and sounder base of candidates entering the revitalized examination program.

This continual increase in candidates—which by the mid-1980s had the Institute administering over 4,000 exams each year—strained two of the Institute's best resources: its staff in Charlottesville and its graders. The 1970s had brought several staffing changes and some expansion. Bea Gordon, who had devoted herself to the Institute for many years, retired in 1976 due to ill health, and died the following year. John Gregg, hired to assist her as Institute registrar, divided Gordon's duties with Peggy Slaughter, Scott Bauman's administrative assistant and later the Institute's business manager. O. Whitfield Broome, who would succeed Bauman as ICFA executive director in 1978, had come on as Examinations Administrator in 1973, a position he retained through 1978. Assisting him was David Croll, like Broome a faculty member at UVa's McIntire School of Commerce; Croll administered the C.I.C. program for the Institute.

Perhaps the most unrelievedly busy staff member from the mid-1970s to the early 1980s was Hartman "Hap" Butler, who as education administrator (1975-77) and then operations director (from 1977 to his retirement in 1983) was the ICFA's first full-time administrator. Butler came to the Institute after a long career with Duff, Anderson and Clark in Chicago, and brought with him not only the experience of a long-time practitioner, but also his own "outstanding" ability to "communicate clearly and effectively with financial analysts," as Robert Milne put it. As Institute administrators had been doing from the start, Butler wore many hats: budget preparer; managing editor of the *CFA Digest*; coordinator of Institute needs and FARF programs; reviewer of CFA study materials for year-to-year changes; liaison to candidate groups and to the Investment Analysis Standards Board, which annually evaluated the appropriateness of CFA I as the FAF fellows qualifying exam; and vice chairman of the Council of Examiners under Brierly Anderson and Jay Vawter. Given the extensiveness of his roles, Butler was, as Pres Brooks, Institute president 1977-78, noted, "the glue that [kept] our act together."

In his capacity as council vice chairman, Butler attended meetings of the Examiners subcommittees, along with Examinations Administrator Whit Broome and the council chairman. Like many of the other examiners, he also attended the summer grading sessions. As candidate enrollments began to swell in the late 1970s and early 1980s, the strains on the grading staff became as apparent as those on the Institute's administrators. From the outset, the CFA program had developed a comprehensive and lengthy grading and review process. The CFA exams were essay rather than multiple choice tests; they probed a candidate's judgment, not just his or her knowledge. Although the CFA I examination had included a multiple choice section beginning in 1972, the examination sequence was still overwhelmingly comprised of essay and case-analysis questions. The answers to such questions were obviously more difficult to evaluate than multiple choice answers, which could be graded by machine.

Since the Institute's clear intent, in Stewart Sheppard's words, was to insure the "relevance, fairness and quality of the examinations," a grading procedure was needed that would be as objective as possible. Every summer the Institute assembled a large grading staff, consisting primarily of practicing CFAs, including trustees and those on the Council of Examiners able to attend. Some non-CFAs from the University of Virginia's business faculty were used, but only for the CFA I examinations. Graders were assigned one question to grade—over and over. In fact, before they ever arrived in Charlottesville they had been sent the question, study materials on that question, and its guideline answer (formerly staff-generated but now written by the Council of Examiners). Graders were expected, in the words of Whit Broome, to become "experts in the topic they would grade."

Once the grading was completed and results tabulated, the Institute senior staff would meet to conduct a review of marginal papers. Then, several weeks later, the Institute trustees assembled in Charlottesville to conduct a further review. This rather complicated process was designed to ensure and verify objectivity and fairness. The explosion of candidates between 1977 and 1982 strained the process, requiring a sizable increase in the number of graders needed, and lengthening the various reviews. In addition, in 1981 the examinations themselves were lengthened by 45 minutes. There was considerable discussion among the Examiners and Trustees about the possibility of expanding the number of multiple choice questions at Level I (which was done), as well as including such questions at the other levels to ease the grading burden. The philosophical consensus of the various Boards of Trustees has been, and continues to be, to keep the CFA examination sequence in essay form, no matter how complex the fair grading of such exams might be.

*   *   *

The ready acceptance of the CFA examination program in the mid-1970s by other elements of the financial industry, such as the ICAA and NYSE, was strong evidence of the Institute's growing stature as an educational standard for the profession. The upgrading of the CFA examination and study program between 1977 and 1982, moreover, demonstrated the Institute's commitment to maintaining its position as industry standard by keeping pace with the rapid, extraordinary changes within the field of financial analysis.

Perhaps most important, the ICFA provided an examination program that did more than test its candidates; it also educated them. From its earliest beginnings in Ezra Solomon's proposal to Abe Kulp's committee, the CFA program was intended to parallel an analyst's actual career. A junior analyst would first learn the tools of his trade; in several years, acting in a staff capacity, he might supervise some junior analysts and be involved in investment decisions; finally, as a senior analyst or manager, the typical analyst might run a research department and most certainly would be involved in decision- and policy-making. With this in mind, Solomon proposed an examination sequence to "guide [analysts] to make a systematic study of subject matter areas which tie in with their work." The early examinations were designed to reflect a candidate's progress in the profession.

Twenty years later, of course, the profession itself had changed so radically that few analysts followed the junior analyst-to-research department sequence. But whether he spent his entire career as a portfolio manager or specialized in analyzing a particular industry, the typical financial analyst experienced a progressive deepening of knowledge and judgment during his career. The CFA examination program still addressed itself to this progression. Where other professional examination programs, even those with multi-year examination sequences, tested their candidates only once on a given subject, the Institute recognized that financial accounting, for example, continued to be used—in increasingly complex ways—as one progressed as a financial analyst, and tested its candidates on such topics at several different levels.

Thus, the work of Jay Vawter and succeeding Council of Examiners chairmen, Robert Puchniak and James LaFleur, to insure the progressive, sequential nature of each topic in the CFA examinations, was a reaffirmation of the Institute's long-time purpose. The Institute might indeed be considered the educational standard in the financial community, not only for the quality of individual exams, but also for the progressive educational sequence it provided its candidates.

CHAPTER TEN
Serving the Membership

Throughout its first decade, the Institute of Chartered Financial Analysts had set for itself the task of establishing a program of professionalization for analysts. Inspired by Benjamin Graham's challenge to the Federation to create a "professional rating" system, the Institute's work was contingent upon the unproven assumption that financial analysis was indeed a profession. While that assumption still stirs some debate 25 years later, Abe Kulp, Stewart Sheppard, and the Institute's founding trustees believed sufficiently in its truth to act. Once the ICFA program was in existence and functioning, there was time to worry about definitions. In fact, during the late 1960s, at both the Institute and the Federation much attention was devoted to recognizing the salient features of a profession—an identifiable body of knowledge, a means for testing that knowledge, an agreed upon and enforced ethical code—and measuring the position of financial analysis against them.

By the early 1970s, the Institute had reached a sufficient degree of surety about its meaning to turn its attention further outward. Thus, the ICFA's second decade was spent less in defining itself than in consolidating its position in the financial community. External circumstances reinforced this outward orientation. Volatile market conditions alarmed investors, who in turn encouraged governmental bodies to scrutinize the industry, particularly its investment advisers and research personnel. The possibility of state or federal regulation loomed large for much of the decade, fueling merger talks between the Institute and Federation, and in a sense forcing the ICFA's hand regarding its professional conduct program. These pressures had a beneficial effect, however; for in establishing a viable program of ethical enforcement, the Institute put itself at the head of the industry and became the standard. When the ICFA's revitalized examination program was accepted by both governmental and investment industry sources in the latter half of the 1970s, its position was further strengthened. Candidates who successfully completed the CFA examination sequence, and who adhered to the Institute's ethical standards, might correctly be judged as having attained the "public warranty" that Stewart Sheppard viewed as the Institute's goal.

But what of the existing members? By 1978, some of them had held charters for 10 or 15 years. In twentieth century America, which lives at an ever-accelerating rate of change, 15 years was akin to decrepitude. Moreover, in the investment business, the period between 1962 and 1978 had seen an explosion in knowledge and consequent revolution in techniques, as well as a dramatic increase in both the number of individual investors and the concentration of institutional investors in the various markets. "Fundamental" analysis might continue to be "fundamentally" the same for some as it had been in 1963; yet what one analyzed, and for whom, were considerably different. Thus by 1979 and 1980, the material on which candidates were tested had changed so dramatically that Institute presidents Roderick O'Neil and William Cornish were wondering aloud whether any of the early charterholders—themselves included—could pass the current examinations.

A substantial gap in knowledge between older and younger CFAs was a likely result of the evolution in investment instruments and practices. Had the Institute any obligation to verify and, if necessary, remedy this situation? Administrators, officers, and trustees considered this question throughout the 1970s. There were two schools of thought on the matter. One, as President O'Neil wrote in August 1978 to Charles Ellis (then chairman of the Continuing Education Committee and later the Institute's twentieth president), viewed "the granting of the Charter as a permanent achievement, somewhat like the granting of an academic degree as a sign of having completed a formal course." The other attitude, O'Neil continued, regarded the charter as "a symbol of professional competence [that] must be earned continuously by assimilation of modern and innovative concepts." O'Neil himself leaned toward the latter point of view, with the expectation that Institute members would soon be encouraged—and perhaps someday required—to participate in continued study. Such a development, O'Neil cautioned, "is not something we should spring on our membership." Rather, "[a] dialogue should be opened, so that the trustees, in the long run, could determine and implement the will of the majority."

That the ICFA should sponsor a continuing education program was not an entirely new thought, of course. As early as 1964, the trustees had considered whether to establish an "ongoing program" for members. In 1971, that questioning became more formalized. Institute president Edmund Mennis set up a committee that year to explore potential continuing education programs. This committee, chaired by Mary Petrie, investigated the possibility of conducting seminars. Financial troubles, however, had effectively precluded any extensive undertaking in that area, beyond the publication of the *CFA Digest.*

When Scott Bauman assumed the directorship in 1972, he came with the intention of fostering continuing education programs. His plans were initially stalled by financial constraints, but by 1974 the Institute was reaching financial stability and could begin to design such activities. Bauman relished the task. He considered himself to be in a crucial position to enhance such programs, because he served as executive director for both the ICFA and the Research Foundation. In Bauman's view, "FARF was a logical vehicle . . . to support a continuing education program for financial analysts as well as for CFA members." As he remembers it, the "synergism between the ICFA and FARF" was at its strongest in 1974-75 when Robert Milne was Institute president. Milne was a business partner of FARF President David Watterson. Their close relationship helped to spark a series of one-day seminars and resulting publications. The smooth administration of these was handled by Bauman, in his dual directorship, and Robert Trent, research administrator of both the Institute and the Foundation.

The first jointly sponsored ICFA-FARF seminar was held at Rice University in Houston, on May 20, 1974. Partially underwritten by a grant from Texas Commerce Bank, the seminar featured a discussion of the efficient capital market and random walk hypotheses. Practitioners were represented on the panel by Frank Block, Edmund Mennis, Jack Treynor, and Jerome Valentine; the academicians were Neil Wright, William Sharpe, and Michael Jensen. Each submitted an essay, which was included in a proceedings volume published the following year. Reflecting back on this publication, Scott Bauman remarked, "our marketing instincts got the best of us and we named this Proceedings Issue, *Is Financial Analysis Useless?*" Despite the pro-EMH sound of the title, the seminar and its proceedings were well received.

Even more successful was the second joint Foundation and Institute seminar, *The Renaissance of Value,* held in New York City in September 1974. The program featured six national figures: Benjamin Graham, John Burr Williams, James Lorie, Arthur Laffer, Frank Block, and Walter Stern. Given the location, the composition of the panel, and the undying interest of analysts in the determination of "value," the program had nearly 400 attendees and was "a huge success."

Seminars continued apace during Bauman's directorship and under the successive ICFA presidencies of Robert Blixt (1975-76), Walter Stern (1976-77) and Philip P. Brooks (1977-78). With the assistance of Research and Publications Committee chairman William Craig, the Institute organized and co-sponsored seminars in Los Angeles and Ottowa (spring and fall, 1975); and in New York, Chicago, and Washington, D.C. (winter, spring, and fall, 1976). Although attendance at any of the Institute's seminars was necessarily limited, the entire ICFA membership participated through the published seminar proceedings, which every CFA received gratis as part of his or her membership privileges. Hap Butler, who during his early years with the Institute was contracted to devote one-third of his time to Research Foundation matters, was responsible for the proceedings issues. Additionally, in fall 1977, the Institute began co-sponsoring executive seminars with Virginia's Darden School, to which only CFAs were invited.

Institute members also received certain volumes in a series of FARF publications called Occasional Papers. Begun in 1974, these publications—known as the FARF Monographs—supplied members with serious, concise presentations of new research in financial analysis and related fields, usually around 100 pages long. Moreover, in 1974 the Institute distributed to members the collected papers of Nicholas Molodovsky. Edited by Robert Milne and entitled *Investment Values in a Dynamic World*, the book was financed in part by a donation from Ed Mennis, the second recipient of the FAF's Nicholas Molodovsky Award. Molodovsky himself, upon receiving the first such award, had given the accompanying stipend to the Research Foundation to sponsor a book on quantitative techniques, later co-authored by Mennis and Jerome Valentine. In 1972, Mennis was able to repay his late mentor by helping to sponsor the eventual publication of Molodovsky's collected works.

By the end of 1977, Institute members had benefited from seven ICFA/FARF seminars and their published proceedings, seven Occasional Papers, and the Molodovsky book. The extensive activity that characterized the period from 1974 to 1977 declined when the officers and staff returned their attention to the examination program. The Institute continued to co-sponsor seminars, occasionally along with the Federation—whose educational programs the ICFA tried not to duplicate—and continued to distribute many FARF publications free to CFAs. However, as Scott Bauman recalls, its close relationship with FARF waned as "a gradual erosion occurred in [their] mutual interests. . . . " In 1975, David Watterson had resigned as FARF president; two years later the FARF board, headed by Watterson's successor Jerome Valentine, accepted an offer from Stewart Sheppard, the Darden School dean, to "staff, house, and service" the Foundation, and moved its office and personnel there.

As discussed in the previous chapter, the Institute's primary focus during the late 1970s shifted to upgrading the study and examination materials of the Candidate Program. Such attention meant that less time was available for the development of the member program. Moreover, Scott Bauman left the Institute in 1978 to return to teaching. His successor, Whit Broome, was by no means uninterested in the continuing education program, but because of his own particular experience and because of administrative needs at the Institute, he was unable to devote much time to the program during his first few years as executive director. Broome had been the examinations administrator since 1973. Prior to that he had, in his capacity as a University of Virginia accounting faculty member, been called upon as an exam grader at Level I and had occasionally written abstracts for the *CFA Digest.* He brought with him considerable knowledge of the CFA Candidate Program, particularly of the Institute's function as exam giver.

The momentum of the continuing education program lessened with the shift of focus to the examination program, but it was not lost. During Philip Brooks' tenure as Institute president (1977-78) the trustees organized their meetings around business pertaining to the "candidate program" and the "member program." This division prefigures the Institute's current administrative structure—the Department of Candidate Programs and the Department of Education and Research. It was becoming undeniable that the Institute had two functions, even if both could not yet be given equal attention.

Brooks' successor, Roderick O'Neil, envisioned a substantial commitment to continuing education. Addressing the Institute members, O'Neil said: "It is my own view that a Charter holder will find it necessary to continue to keep educated on developments within the profession and that it will be in the interest of all members of the Institute that this process be more formalized than it is at the moment."

At the beginning of Whit Broome's tenure, O'Neil had written to him concerning the ICFA's objectives. Besides hoping to increase the Institute's visibility in the industry and attain a "frank and productive dialogue with the FAF" about their respective roles, O'Neil believed that the Institute would "have to incorporate some continuing education activities as a part of the responsibility of a Charter holder." O'Neil hoped to have the issue "defined" during the coming year, but recognized that the program could not be imposed on the membership; it must be discussed with them rather than handed down from on high.

The parameters of such a program were investigated by the Continuing Education Committee, which was headed by Charles Ellis between 1976 and 1980. Ever since continuing education for members was first explored seriously, in the early 1970s, a major concern of the Institute was to avoid overlapping or duplicating FAF activities. Before the Institute had come into existence, the Federation had been sponsoring educational activities, both in the form of luncheon talks at the local society level and the Beloit (later Rockford) summer seminars. The Institute itself was an educational outgrowth of the Federation. Although technically a separate organization, for many years the ICFA was viewed in a proprietary way by many within the FAF. For their part, Institute trustees and administrators acknowledged their philosophical— and earlier financial—debt to the Federation, even while feeling zealous about the Institute's independence.

By the late 1970s, the FAF had increased its educational activities considerably over what was being done early in the ICFA's history. In expanding its education program, the FAF in effect strengthened its industry position and helped to heal wounds opened during the years of dissension with the NYSSA. There was much talk among the Institute's trustees about how best to serve their members without duplicating the Federation's educational efforts. In May 1977, Charles Ellis reported to the board on the possibility of joining the FAF "in the sponsoring of a Continuing Education Program." Ellis worked with the Federation's Russ Mason on this possibility. The immediate outcome of this liaison was a series of seminars held at the FAF's annual convention each spring, deemed to be of interest to CFAs and CFA candidates. These did not prove attractive enough to the membership to constitute a real continuing education program, and efforts to establish one languished.

Throughout the late 1970s and early 1980s, the only genuine vehicle for the continuing education of members remained the *CFA Digest*. Edited by Ed Mennis (who in 1978 became the third recipient of the C. Stewart Sheppard Award) and managed by

Hap Butler, the quarterly kept members current on academic and practitioner developments in the profession. Between 1976 and 1980, Butler remembers, "steps were taken to strengthen and expand" the *Digest*. New abstractors were hired, new journals were added as potential sources of article abstracts, and greater emphasis was placed on "investment analysis and portfolio management." In addition, the overall number of articles abstracted increased from 20 to close to 30. By increasing the flow of articles circulating between abstractors and Institute, Butler and Mennis had been able to eliminate quickly those articles unworthy of consideration and to give the abstractors more time to devote to those to be included. The result was a stronger publication that served the continuing educational needs of members until a formal program could be undertaken.

*   *   *

By the fall of 1981 the Institute was ready to make "a major and sustained commitment to continuing education for members and the profession." After years of inchoately recognizing the desirability of such an effort, the trustees and administration were prepared to formalize their plans. The coalescence of several factors had brought them to this point. Perhaps most important was the obvious need: those who had held their charters for 10 years or more were in danger of becoming, as Nicholas Molodovsky had warned a decade earlier, "illiterate" in their own profession. Moreover, by 1981 the sheer number of charterholders dwarfed that of candidates; there were just under 2,000 in the examination program that year, while nearly 7,000 men and women held charters. The ICFA had an undeniable obligation to provide educational services for them that were not available elsewhere. Happily, by 1981 the Institute had the financial wherewithal to underwrite the cost of creating and organizing such services. Finally, it had in place leaders convinced of the necessity of continuing education. James R. Vertin, Institute president in 1981-82, brought with him a clear recognition of the ICFA's dual function as exam-giver for candidates and educator for members. He was determined to emphasize the latter function. Moreover, Trustee Charles Ellis had long been interested in the continuing education for members. Ellis had chaired the Institute's Continuing Education Committee for several years, and more recently had headed the Members Program Task Force of the Long-Range Planning Committee formed by Alfred C. Morley during his term as ICFA president the previous year.

Ellis' task force had in fact opened the "dialogue with the membership" envisioned by Rory O'Neil in 1979. With the help of Whit Broome the task force first reviewed the Institute's existing services to members, which at the time consisted of mailing free of charge the *CFA Digest*, selected FARF monographs, a directory and newsletters. The Institute also co-sponsored occasional seminars and symposia, like the Mortgage-Backed Bond and Pass-Through Symposium of 1979. The Members Program Task Force next prepared a preliminary report for James Vertin, the vice president under Morley, who coordinated the Long-Range Planning work. In it they proposed to examine other learned professions to see what—if any—continuing education activities they conducted and to "informally survey" a small sample of CFAs deemed leaders in the profession "asking for guidance on broad subject areas to cover. . . . " Finally, they would send questionnaires to a large number of CFAs to "measure the members' views" on continuing education, its probable cost, its probable nature (mandatory or voluntary), and the areas of its greatest impact. From its own consensual viewpoint, Ellis' task force agreed that both the rapid changes in the profession and the diverse interests—and hence professional specialties—of analysts ought to be addressed by any formal Institute continuing education program.

By June 1981 Ellis' committee had compiled the results of their first "dialogue" with CFAs and completed their survey of other professions. "Relative to its peer groups," the task force reported, "the Institute has very low dues and a low level of continuing education." Other professions had developed extensive member programs, some of them mandatory. To fill this gap in the profession of financial analysis, the task force recommended that "the Institute devote its resources and capabilities to collecting, upgrading, teaching and testing on existing knowledge," rather than originating new knowledge (more properly the mission of the FARF). The range of subjects to be collected, upgraded and disseminated included "types of *investments*," — particularly newer vehicles like options, futures, real estate and international investments; "type of *investors*" — "individuals, endowments, foundations, pension funds (both private and public)" and the like; as well as the "basic *issues*" in investment decision-making — "asset allocation, long-term objective setting, managing an investment research organization, inflation, application of MPT, and use of information technology." Finally, the task force suggested the development of courses, either for home study or for groups, on areas of interest to CFAs: accounting, SEC and other regulations and laws, management problems, corporate finance. The Institute's proposed continuing education program was going to have quite an extensive menu.

As for the dues increase, Ellis' task force was cautious. Their initial small sample of active CFAs had shown both a strong endorsement of a continuing education program and a willingness to pay higher dues to support it. A later, more general survey of CFAs would show the same. This was not really surprising. Since its beginnings in 1963, the Institute had only once increased members' dues, raising them from $25 to $35 in 1972. Paying $35 for membership in a professional organization that provided member services — even on a limited basis — was a notable bargain by the 1980s. Despite the CFAs' support for a long overdue increase, Ellis' committee recommended that any dues increase be postponed until one year *after* the implementation of a continuing education program. Members should be convinced they were getting something in return for their dues.

Armed with the Long-Range Planning Subcommittee's report on the development of a members' program, Institute president Jim Vertin approached the Board of Trustees in September 1981. Vertin and Ellis summarized the task force's findings including the questionnaires sent to two separate samples of members which showed CFA support for continuing education. To finance such a program Vertin asked for a continuing education budget of $40,000. But the trustees didn't agree. Instead, they voted for a three-year commitment to continuing education with an annual budget of $150,000. In fact, as Vertin remembers it, "they wouldn't let me out of the room until they'd given me $150,000."

Ellis and Vertin felt, and the Trustees concurred, that the first order of business in establishing a formal program of continuing education for members was to create a new ICFA staff position, director of continuing education, and hire someone to fill it. Although a number of candidates were considered, the eventual director was found at the Institute itself, Darwin M. Bayston, who in 1980 had filled the newly created position of programs director. Himself a CFA, Bayston had brought with him 10 years' experience as both practitioner and academic, having taught part time at Illinois State while working at a trust company. The position of "Programs Director" superceded on a full-time basis that of examination administrator, which had been part time when held by Whit Broome and his successors. As programs director, Bayston had been responsible for supervising the registration and enrollment of candidates, working with both the Council of Examiners and the Research and Publications Committee, overseeing the complex grading process—including staff and trustee reviews, and assisting the perennially busy Hap Butler with the ever more detailed candidate questionnaires and the annual publication of the three *CFA Study Guides*. In these various capacities Bayston had done "a *superb* job" according to Charles Ellis, and could be expected "to get the continuing education program off to a fast and effective start."

Bayston took over as the director of continuing education in January 1982, although until a director of candidate programs was appointed the following June he continued to work on the examination program. To oversee the philosophical direction of the Continuing Education Program that Darwin Bayston was to administer, Vertin and the trustees created a volunteer council on continuing education composed of academics and practitioners, both CFAs and non-CFAs. Appointed in May 1982, the first Council on Continuing Education (CCE) consisted of Bayston, Ellis, Vertin, Dean LeBaron, James von Germeten (all CFAs), and the academicians Roger Murray, Jay Light, Larry Selden and Stephen Ross. The CCE held its first meeting on June 23, 1982, during which it formally stated its mission, defined the roles in which it "acts with the Director" and discussed the various topics for seminars that Darwin Bayston had been investigating. The CCE saw that its mission was to identify "areas of developing knowledge" in the field of financial analysis and to organize such knowledge in "programs, publications and in audio-visual forms" for dissemination to "CFAs, candidates, and others, so they [could] maintain and enhance their professional expertise and effectiveness." The Council also charged itself with reviewing and guiding the long-range strategy for the Continuing Education Program, and its frequent reevaluation. They also hoped to help identify individuals who could and would contribute to the programs. Among those consulted by Bayston on the Council's recommendation were Donald Tuttle and George Noyes on the topic of fixed-income securities, and on the topic of accounting, former Institute president Frank Block, the recipient of the 1979 C. Stewart Sheppard Award and a member of the Financial Accounting Standards Board.

On October 26 and 27, 1982, the Institute held its first continuing education seminar, *Management Skills for Investment Managers,* in Washington, D.C. The seminar panel, which included Dave H. Williams, Richard Boylan, Harold Arbit, Daniel Forrestal, Paul Miller and Richard Cosier, discussed topics ranging from common management strategies to factors unique to the investment business. Of the 105 participants at the seminar, 75 returned seminar evaluations; most rated the sessions above-average in overall usefulness—welcome news to Bayston and the CCE, who were themselves in the process of learning how to present educational programs for financial professionals. Published proceedings of the seminar, edited by James Vertin, were distributed to members early in 1983. The Institute received a considerable number of favorable comments on this publication, and soon the Council was planning "a related program," possibly for the fall of 1983.

Recognizing the probable "confluence of interest" between the FAF, ICFA and FARF, Council members Jim Vertin and Walter Stern recommended that the three groups "look for opportunities to share and cooperate together." The first example of this cooperation was in February 1983, when the Institute and

Federation held two days of seminars on *Microcomputers: Automating the Analyst and Portfolio Manager.* Because the 225 attendees brought with them "a wide range of knowledge and expectation," their satisfaction with the program as an educational experience varied. While most felt the speakers' presentations were valuable and the discussions that followed interesting, the overall assessment was that the exhibits part of the program was not sufficiently educational. No proceedings were issued.

Perhaps the most successful of the initial seminars was that held in New York, February 3-4, 1983, on *The Revolution in Techniques for Managing Bond Portfolios.* According to Bayston, the program "exceeded all expectations in terms of attendance and program content." Over 200 people attended, with another 100 turned away because of space limitations. The program was rated so highly that the Institute repeated it in San Francisco at the end of March. Its proceedings, edited by Don Tuttle, were distributed to members in early May.

Thus, within a year of its founding, the Institute's Council on Continuing Education had sponsored three seminars, repeated one, and issued two volumes of proceedings. Within another year, four more followed, along with published proceedings: *Managing the Investment Professional,* edited by James Vertin; *Options and Futures,* edited by Donald E. Fischer; *Improving the Investment Decision Process,* edited by H. Russell Fogler and Darwin Bayston; and *International Equity Investing,* also edited by Vertin. In a very short time the ICFA had established a viable program of continuing education for its members, what Rory O'Neil had once called "an important part of the Institute's pursuit of its basic professional responsibilities." Most gratifying to all involved, the program was being enthusiastically received.

Besides sponsoring seminars, the Institute had undertaken publication of volumes it thought pertinent to members' continuing education. Annually since 1983, it has presented to members a publication entitled *The CFA Candidate Study and Examination: A Review.* Taking as a point of departure the view held by former presidents O'Neil and Cornish, among others, that those who had attained their charters more than 10 years previous would find it difficult—if not impossible—to pass the current CFA examinations, the *Review* book gave members a chance to familiarize themselves with the content of the most recent examinations and related study materials. Because the book reprinted all three levels of the most recent exams (along with guideline answers), CFAs could measure their knowledge against that required of current candidates. The Institute also sent out in 1984 a *Summary of Proceedings, 1976-82* of the Institute for Quantitative Research in Finance. Also, *Managing Investment Portfolios: A Dynamic Process,* edited by John Maginn and Donald Tuttle, had been enthusiastically received by members a year earlier and was contributing substantially to their ongoing professional education.

In August 1985, the ICFA went a step further in its Continuing Education Program, establishing a formal, though voluntary, program of member accreditation. Long discussed by Institute officers and trustees, and investigated in detail by a committee headed by trustee Kathleen Condon, the impetus for an accreditation program actually came from members in response to a series of general questionnaires that were sent out between the fall of 1983 and the spring of 1985. The practice of surveying CFAs had begun on an ad hoc basis during Jim Vertin's term as president (1981-82). During the January 1982 trustees meeting the officers (Vertin, Vice President Robert Morrison and Secretary-Treasurer Charles Ellis) introduced a motion, which passed, that rescinded the specific education and experience requirements for candidates. As the February *CFA Newsletter* reported to members, the step was taken "in recognition of the Institute's success in developing a comprehensive written body of professional knowledge and an effective series of examinations with which to test the knowledge of candidates." Vertin also announced the change and requested comments in a letter sent to members on April 19, 1982. The members responded. In fact, nearly 50 percent responded, an extraordinarily high sample, and they didn't like the change. As a result, the board, though still favoring the decision to drop requirements, reversed itself, and took an object lesson from the experience: in the future members would be surveyed.

The opening of this formalized dialogue with Institute members meant that no action on accreditation would be taken until their opinions were solicited. As part of three surveys, members were asked to rate existing programs (seminars, journals, other publications), and to indicate their feelings about whether an accreditation program should be required or optional. Seventy-one percent of the Institute's responding charterholders indicated that continuing education via accreditation should be either mandatory or highly encouraged. In their responses, ICFA members expressed, as John Maginn and Alfred Morley wrote in announcing the accreditation program, "a strong desire for an educational program that will help them maintain excellence as investment professionals." Moreover, they continued,

> In equally strong terms, members have indicated that such a program be voluntary, practical, and designed so that participants can select areas and subjects of their own professional interest from a broad list of appropriate educational activities. Finally, members also have suggested that professional recognition be given to those participating in a meaningful way.

In less than four years, the idea of continuing education to assure the maintenance of professional standards had gone from possibility to reality. As Jim Vertin reminded the Council on Continuing Education, the Institute had good reason to feel gratified to observe so soon "the transition of the hopes of 1982 into the tangible accomplishments that have been recorded."

CHAPTER ELEVEN
Planning the Future

The planning and implementation of a continuing education program undertaken by the staff, officers and trustees betokened both a new level of commitment to furthering professionalism and a new direction for the ICFA in the 1980s. The need to get the Institute functioning was so pressing in the early years that Stewart Sheppard and Ray Smith, professionals themselves but new to the exam-giving process, had to improvise policies and procedures as they went. In the middle years, the trustees and administrators were interested in defining the profession of financial analysis and its relation to other professions as well as to the investment business as a whole. They needed to determine what the ICFA's role should be in the entire process of professionalization. By the early 1980s, however, the Institute was not so much asking "what are we doing?" as "where are we going?" Its position of prominence as *the* professional organization in the investment business brought with it both new responsibilities and the danger of complacency.

Perhaps no one saw this danger more keenly than Alfred C. "Pete" Morley, the Institute's incoming president in the spring of 1980. Morley had been active in Institute committee work since the early 1970s, serving throughout the decade on the Professional Ethics Committee and from 1975 on the Council of Examiners. In the same year he became a trustee and had thus been in a position to observe and assist in the Institute's growing stature within the industry. Morley had likewise witnessed the continual review and updating needed to keep the ICFA at the forefront of the profession. Although by 1980 the Institute no longer depended on the improvisational approach of the early years, Morley felt a surer sense of direction could be achieved. In April 1980, he wrote the Institute officers to that effect:

> Our organization has made enormous strides over the seventeen years of its existence and there is absolutely no doubt that further considerable progress can and will be achieved. However, it seems to me that a more detailed map and compass now are needed to help assure achievement of that progress.

To that end, Morley proposed the formation and adequate funding of a Long-Range Planning Committee whose function would be to answer the question, "what is our long-term goal?" for each of the five specific areas. Such answers, Morley expected, would be precise enough "to define exactly what the [Institute] might hope to be if all of its internal resources are used in the best possible way and in full consideration of the constraints and limits imposed by external influences." Evaluation of external conditions was necessary, Morley suggested, to avoid short-sighted complacency:

> We too often tend to assume that society and the economy will continue to support our growth and operation in more or less the same way they have in the past. Yet in the world of the 1980's, this is clearly not a valid assumption ... [when] every organization in the world is more structured and limited each day by what is happening around it. Failure to assess the probable impact of the external environment on the organization can be disastrous.

The trustees approved Morley's suggestion at their April meeting and James R. Vertin, the Institute's vice president, agreed to head the planning project. His initial concern was to find the best people to lead task forces in the five designated areas of Institute planning: organization and finance, external relations, headquarters, candidate program, and member program. By late summer the leaders were set: Walter McConnell, Roderick O'Neil, Walter Stern, William Cornish and Charles Ellis, respectively. The planning project's intent, Morley cautioned, was not to diminish "the success of the past and the positive momentum of the present," but rather to attend to the Institute's responsibility "to the now many thousands of members and the many hundreds in the candidate program to assure our contracted support to their ongoing professional achievement."

In order to generate, in Vertin's words, the kind of "useful, sensible work [needed] to move the organization into the future effectively," a shaking of the foundations was necessary. At the beginning of each subcommittee's work no Institute policy or procedure was to be considered too sacred to question: not the by-laws, not the ethical enforcement program, not the grading process, not the selection of trustees, not the Institute's location, not the fee structure, not even the examination sequence itself ("should there be an Examination IV?" Bill Cornish's task force was asked).

On January 21, 1981, Vertin and Broome met with the five task force chairmen, each of whom submitted a preliminary report. In general, the task forces had looked carefully at the Institute and found it sound—but not perfect. The headquarters in Charlottesville were considered adequate for another five years; the affiliation with the University was no longer "necessary" as it had been to a fledgling ICFA 20 years earlier; the possibility of a full-time director was worth contemplating, though that presented problems for Whit Broome who could become full time only at the cost of his academic tenure. Other potential changes were considered: means of further cooperation with the FAF in addition to their joint committees (PEC/IASB and Professional Conduct) and joint ethics questionnaires; ways of better utilizing the Financial Analysts Research Foundation; the possibility of establishing an Institute endowment; the development of various specialty exams to supplement the existing three. Perhaps most pressing of all was the recommendation of the Members Program

Task Force that the Institute make a major commitment to a continuing education program.

The January 1981 meeting marked the close of the first phase of Morley's long-range planning initiative. This phase, as Morley and Vertin envisioned it, was to be one of information-gathering. Next would come evaluation; finally action. Thus had each of the five task force subcommittees consulted with Whit Broome about existing structures, finances, and policies. In February, Roderick O'Neil wrote his External Relations unit what might have been said to four of the five groups: "Our work is done. . . . Our group is now disbanded. Never again say that nothing is ever ended."

Phases of movement may end, but momentum itself continues. Sometimes, of course, the direction changes. Instead of going into a general evaluative phase, Morley's long-range planning strategy was diverted by the urgent need to implement a continuing education program. As detailed in the previous chapter, Charles Ellis and the Members Program Task Force brought in a strong recommendation that the Institute make "a major commitment" to establishing such a program "effective immediately." Their program was further strengthened by CFA surveys that indicated considerable support for continuing education from the members. As we have seen under Morley's successor James Vertin, the program was begun with the hiring of Darwin Bayston as its director and the selecting of possible seminar topics. Robert W. Morrison, who succeeded Vertin and was the Institute's second Canadian president, saw the actual implementation of a continuing education program during his term of office (1982-83).

Morrison's tenure as president also saw the beginnings of a second strategic planning initiative. The five original task forces had been disbanded, but their work was furthered by a two-member committee consisting of trustee Gary Burkhead and Jay Vawter, secretary-treasurer under Morrison. In January 1982 the two presented the board with an interim planning report, which was intended to continue "the outstanding effort instigated by Pete Morley and carried out by Jim Vertin." Vawter and Burkhead's report addressed large issues rather than specific operational details. The report was especially concerned that the Institute's officers and administrators define specifically both long-range goals ("what we want to look like five years from now") and short-term planning activities ("we want to develop a sense of focus that is practical and decision-oriented rather than merely an academic exercise that leads to no action and ultimately just fades away"). Also important was to determine the nature of the long-range planning itself. Should it be an "ongoing, open-ended, never-ending process" or a major, "periodic" effort?

Leading the discussion that followed the report was Charles Ellis, the Institute's vice president. Long a proponent of such forward thinking, Ellis suggested that in setting both early and long-range goals, the officers should meet, make decisions and present them to the trustees for discussion and action. Agreeing with this, the trustees designated a committee consisting of the present officers, Morrison, Ellis and Vawter, and the incoming secretary-treasurer, John Maginn, to begin to study such practical short-term planning strategies as the need for a full-time executive director, and the possible relocation of the Institute, whose headquarters were becoming increasingly cramped. At the board's next meeting, May 15, 1983, the work of this committee was formally recognized and added to the by-laws as the Executive Committee of the Institute, whose function, according to Whit Broome, would be "to deal with operating matters so that the trustees could concentrate on policy and planning matters."

One operating matter put to the Executive Committee at the previous meeting was the question of having a full-time director. As noted earlier, this possibility was difficult for Whit Broome, given his academic career. Yet Broome could recognize that having a full-time director would enhance the professionalization of the Institute staff, a task that had occupied him since he first took over the directorship in September 1978. At that time, the only full-time staff3member was Hartman Butler. Though a dedicated worker, Butler was nearly seventy and beginning to think about a gradual retirement. Broome added Darwin Bayston to the staff in 1980 as a full-time programs director, a position which incorporated the previous part-time examinations administrator role and some of Butler's duties, regarding *Study Guides* and the Research and Publications Committee's work. In 1982, Bayston moved to the new position of director of continuing education. The void this created in the candidate program was filled in July 1982 with the establishment of a parallel position to Bayston's, the director of candidate programs, originally held by Douglas Leathem. Positions for executive assistants to both directors were also created. A year later an office administrator, Robert Luck, was added. In May 1983, Whit Broome agreed to take a one-year leave of absence from his faculty position at Virginia and become the ICFA's first full-time director.

With Whit Broome accepting for a year the full-time executive directorship, the Institute staff was reaching a completely professional level. Such a development augured the eventual lessening of trustee involvement in general operating matters and their heightened attention to long-range goals and policies. To stimulate thinking and reach a consensus on these goals, the incoming Institute president Charles Ellis had solicited letters from the trustees and senior staff containing their thoughts on long-term areas of activity for the ICFA (long-term meaning "by 1990 or even 2000"), upgrading or expanding present areas, and on any currently needed organizational or procedural changes. Predictably, their opinions were contradictory, especially in regard to the respective roles of the Federation, Institute and Research Foundation; equally predictable was the thoughtfulness with which the officers and other trustees considered the Institute's present needs and future goals.

To follow up and expand on these ideas, Ellis appointed a Planning Committee consisting of trustees James von Germeten, chairman, Kathleen Condon and Daniel Forrestal. This three-member committee submitted a preliminary report in September 1983, which was discussed by the trustees, revised and resubmitted in September 1984. A final draft of their *Strategic Plan: 1984-1985* was approved by the rest of the Board on April 29, 1984. The plan defined the ICFA's mission as the development and achievement of strategic goals within four areas: the candidate program—including accreditation; the member program—including conduct, ethics, and the external industry perception of the Institute; the ICFA's relations with the FAF and FARF; and the organizational and financial structure of the

Institute's administration. In addition to setting out the Institute's purposes in each of these four areas, the von Germeten committee proposed some specific "action steps," the first of which was to have one trustee made responsible for "definition, development and achievement" of each of the agreed upon objectives. Among the proposed objectives were formation of an accreditation program, "elevation of the industry's professional image to the total investment community, regulators and the general public," budget and location considerations, and the effecting of a "maximum integration of services" among the three financial analyst organizations.

Recently, that Strategic Plan has been updated by a committee consisting of trustees Daniel Forrestal, chairman, Gary Brinson, and Eugene Sit. Their report, approved by the Board of Trustees in January 1986, cited the progress made in areas recommended by the earlier planning document. Particularly notable was the commitment to accreditation "leading to the normal award of a Certificate of Professional Achievement," and an initiative towards the Financial Analysts Federation that resulted "in joint mission statements and the articulation of key future strategies for both organizations." The report also contained recommended plans of action in five strategic areas: continuing education/accreditation, public awareness, organizational structure in light of the Institute's growth, evaluation of candidate curriculum and examination programs, and international outreach.

*   *   *

The culmination of such long-range thinking, of course, is action. As had been the case with the continuing education program whose establishment was fueled by Pete Morley's planning initiative, several ideas were put into effect even as the planning process evolved. One area immediately addressed was the role of the trustees, given the increasing professionalization of the staff. Trustees now were able to devote more time to broad issues, less to operational details. To facilitate this, Charles Ellis suggested that staff and committee reports, which previously had been read at board meetings, be submitted in writing, in advance, and discussed only when trustees had specific questions. This policy was adopted and put into effect in the spring of 1983, at Robert Morrison's last board meeting as ICFA president.

If the trustees were to be free of most operational decisions, then the executive director's role would likewise have to change. Although devoted to the Institute, Whit Broome did not wish to permanently sever his ties to academia; in fact, he desired to return to full-time teaching and indicated in the spring his intention to do so that fall. Broome agreed to stay on in a part-time capacity, acting as an advisor to his successor. In particular, he would remain active on ethics and conduct matters, providing the initial review of any "questionable" ethics questionnaires and instituting investigations where necessary. As he had been doing as director, Broome would continue to monitor regulatory activities that might have an effect upon the Institute's program of self-regulation. Finally, in his role as a member of the Investment Analysis Standards Board, Broome would act as liaison between that body and the Institute's Professional Ethics Committee, which jointly produced the *Standards of Practice Handbook.*

The impending change in leadership brought about by Broome's altered status, together with the revised role of the officers and trustees, provided an opportunity to redefine the director's functions while searching for Broome's successor. The task of doing so fell to Jay Vawter, at the time vice president under Ellis. Vawter saw the directorship as becoming less an administrative function than an executive one. To be sure, this transformation of role was already taking place during Broome's last and only full-time year, particularly as he became more involved in planning issues. But Vawter foresaw the need for an even greater "executive" function; the director's role should be to "promote" as well as run the Institute.

As Vawter recalls, "there was general agreement among the trustees that this individual might best be a well-known leader from the profession. . . . " Although "a number of very good names surfaced," Vawter had one in mind from the outset—Pete Morley. Distinguished within the profession, long active in Institute matters, a recent officer and still a trustee, Morley also had been thinking determinedly about the ICFA's future for several years, and encouraging others to do so. Moreover, Morley's thinking centered on the need to enhance the Institute's visibility within the industry and with the investing public by ensuring a correct perception of its responsibilities and achievements. This was a concern shared by the trustees—and by the membership, as extensive member surveys in 1983 and 1984 confirmed.

Initially amenable to the idea of becoming the Institute's leader, Morley twice turned down the position when faced with the reality of a cross-country relocation to fill a still somewhat amorphous position. Vawter did not easily accept Morley's refusal. Instead he turned to the trustees for assistance and remembers "spending hours on the phone on Sunday afternoons discussing the whole subject with various officers and other trustees." Finally, at a meeting in Washington, D.C., in the spring of 1984 the negotiations bore fruit: the ICFA executive director's job was redefined as that of a president and chief executive officer—which became its official title; the new role would be that of a corporate officer, not an academic administrator. Morley accepted the position, to which he was unanimously elected by the trustees.

The change in title from executive director to president paralleled changes in the officers' designations as well. At the April 29, 1984 board meeting, the trustees had voted to alter the officers' titles to chairman and vice chairman. The reasoning behind this, according to outgoing "president" Charles Ellis, was that the Institute, which had "moved rapidly from being a small, uncertain, new and not yet accepted enterprise two decades ago, toward being one with . . . a large and strong constituency needing its valuable services," should now be "steering away from being considered a trade association." The restructuring of staff and officer roles would be one way to accomplish this.

Perhaps the most crucial aspect of Morley's new role was that of communication, both with the Institute's members and with the industry at large. The ICFA's desire to open a "dialogue with the membership" had been transformed into action with the establishment of annual surveys. These in turn had informed the officers about areas for further action, including most prominently the accreditation program. At the prompting of Chairman Jay Vawter, the trustees decided to produce an *Annual Report* to inform the membership in detail of the Institute's financial and organizational structures. President Morley had the first report ready for distribution to the membership in late 1984.

Under Morley and Vawter the Institute also expanded its outreach to members and candidates at the local level, continuing a series of visits to FAF societies begun during Whit Broome's year as full-time director. The visits were intended, in Vawter's view, to open up a discussion on a wide range of topics, particularly centered on the CFA program. The Institute wished to be more helpful to the local societies in developing educational programs. The Institute leaders, Morley, Vawter and John Maginn, were especially concerned to visit societies that had extensive educational programs already in place, like that of the Boston Society. Moreover, when the accreditation program was being set up, Morley, Bayston and others visited a number of societies including those in Chicago, New York, Los Angeles, San Francisco, Boston, Richmond, Toronto, Montreal, Houston and San Antonio, to present specific information on that program to members.

The annual member surveys in 1983 and 1984 had verified an opinion long held by Morley. Those responding were dissatisfied with the ICFA's visibility within the investment community. The general feeling expressed was that the profile of the Institute was far too low. Efforts to correct this had begun two years earlier with visits to the annual meetings of the Financial Management Association in 1982 and 1983, which informed their membership about the Institute's activities. Such information was also disseminated to other groups within the financial community, including the office of the Comptroller of the Currency and the College of Financial Planners. Under Morley the Institute's visibility increased, with general informational letters being sent to members, employers, regulators, the financial press, federation members and CFA candidates, each accompanied by the Institute's *Annual Report.* Articles by Morley and others began appearing in the financial press.

In the fall of 1984 the Institute's efforts at becoming better known, via a deliberate policy of publicity and outreach moved into a new phase. In October of that year Chairman Jay Vawter was invited to the Madrid Conference of the European Financial Analysts, "both to be a speaker, representing the Institute" and to become "more acquainted with the foreign analyst community." Vawter found that there was considerable interest in the ICFA among the officials of the various European societies, and "decided it was time for the Institute to take a formal step into the international arena." As a result, the Institute's International Committee was formed in early 1985. In June 1985 the committee determined that as an initial step, formal contact be made with various organizations around the world for the purpose of exchanging ideas and appropriate literature, as well as to research possible cooperative ventures.

The first major effort in this regard was made by Institute President Morley in the summer of 1985, when he visited three cities in India, as well as Singapore and Tokyo. Morley found his contacts in these countries to have "the highest regard for the Institute and its programs," and to be seeking "closer collaboration between the Institute and their respective organizations, all aimed at eventual true globalization of the CFA designation." Intended not to compete with local programs abroad, but rather to enhance them, the Institute's role would center around pursuing such collaboration. As a follow-up to this initial overture, Morley made a subsequent trip to India early in 1986, which also included stops in Singapore, Australia and New Zealand to visit with CFAs about their and the Institute's programs. These trips, as well as efforts by Jay Vawter, John Maginn and others, are leading, according to Vawter, "to improving relationships and an expanding international participation in the Institute's programs." The Institute's relationship with the European analyst community has shown great promise. In October 1985 Jay Vawter and leaders of both the Society of Investment Analysts and the European Federation of Financial Analyst Societies held a dinner meeting at one of London's great old clubs, the Garrick Club. There, they discussed the shrinking economic and financial world and the importance of taking steps, in Vawter's words, "to enhance the quality of the profession worldwide through careful cooperation in terms of education, certification and continuing education." Out of this meeting came plans for a joint seminar held May 1, 1986, in London, on the topic of the impact of regulatory change on the financial industry. The good feeling of cooperation that this preliminary work has generated suggests a new era of expanding influence for the Institute.

EPILOGUE

THE INSTITUTE AS INDUSTRY STANDARD

It is impossible to hold this job [of ICFA President] without recognizing how much is owed to the past. One enters the job surrounded by a structure, by able people, by precedents and a wise set of rules and procedures, and by the existence of goals and momentum that already have the whole thing moving down a constructive path.

James R. Vertin
18th ICFA President
May 1982

If, as William Cornish once suggested, a "Rip Van Winkle, CFA, Class of 1963 would have trouble passing the [1980s'] examinations," it is equally unlikely that any of the original trustees, awakening from a similar slumber, would recognize the Institute they helped to found and whose policies they formed. Instead of a part-time director with one assistant and two file drawers, today's ICFA has a full-time president and chief executive officer in Pete Morley, a vice president and two assistant vice presidents for Education and Research (Darwin Bayston, Cathryn Kittell, and Susan Martin), a vice president and assistant vice president for Candidate Programs (Thomas Bowman and Peggy Slaughter), a full-time treasurer (Robert Luck), a controller (Jane Birckhead), and 25 other full-time administrative and support personnel. Even with electronic filing, the Institute no longer fits on the mezzanine in Monroe Hall. Instead, in February of 1986, the staff moved into the Institute's fourth headquarters, more than ever a corporate headquarters fit for a large and growing organization.

Yet, despite this enormous transformation, no one with a sense of history can think everything changed. If the Institute now has a globe-trotting executive in Pete Morley, it had, in Stewart Sheppard 20 years before, a director who criss-crossed the country with the same purpose in mind: to promote the CFA program. Both have had spectacular results. That 2,010 candidates sat for the fourth CFA examinations some 20 years ago in 1966 was a success beyond Sheppard's or Abe Kulp's wildest imaginings; the over 6,000 registered for 1986—several hundred of whom are from outside the United States and Canada—is equally a cause for pleased astonishment.

Perhaps the differences between 1963 and 1986 are more matters of degree than substance. A two-page Code of Ethics and Guidelines have given way to a 120-page *Standards of Practice Handbook*, it is true. But the commitment to professional ethics has been firm since the Federation's old Professional Ethics and Standards Committee persuaded the directors to found an Institute of Chartered Financial Analysts. Likewise unswerving has been the ICFA's determination to set and maintain uncompromisingly high standards in what Jay Vawter called "the real heart of the Institute"—the exam program. If continuing education and accreditation look brand new, it is well to remember that the impulse behind them is the same as that which drove the Federation's leaders in the late 1950s: an unshakable resolve to establish the validity of financial analysis as a profession. Their determination and that of the hundreds of officers, trustees, committee volunteers and administrative staff members who followed, have ensured that the Institute which exists today—though expanded beyond anyone's dreams—is as "adamant" about professionalism and high standards as Abe Kulp insisted it be 25 years ago.

AFTERWORD

The Institute's growth and influence have far exceeded the modest expectations of the founders. These accomplishments during the past 25 years are a testimony to those many hundreds of volunteers who have served on the Board of Trustees, the committees, and the staff, as well as to the candidates and members. With growing interest in the professionalization of the investment business around the world, the potential for the Institute as a leader in this field is great. Furthermore, given the dynamics of the investment business—its growth and its complexity—a need exists for a comprehensive and contemporary body of knowledge—a role that the Institute is uniquely qualified to fulfill.

Looking forward from our vantage point here in 1986, the Institute can be described as an organization that is really beginning to hit its "stride," like the long distance runner or the developing corporate enterprise. There is a sense of accomplishment, but more importantly a sense of anticipation regarding what the future holds. The Institute has been and must continue to be willing and able to meet these challenges.

During the past five years, the trustees have shaped the Institute to maintain its commitment to professional competence in a more complex and global environment. Those steps have largely been documented in the last six chapters of this history.

To keep pace with this growth and provide for the future, the Institute moved into new and expanded quarters in Charlottesville in the spring of 1986. At the dedication, John Templeton, a CFA and world-renowned investment manager, championed the role of world-wide investing as a means of increasing prosperity and harmony. He challenged the Institute and its members to assume expanded ethical leadership in business throughout the world and to strive for higher and higher standards of professionalism.

Global, international, and world-wide are terms that are being applied to the investment markets and the investment decision-making process. Twenty-four hour trading, geographic diversification and standardized, or more appropriately harmonized or integrated, accounting and regulation are topical subjects in professional journals and trade publications.

The Institute is pioneering in this area with co-sponsorship of seminars, having co-sponsored a seminar in London in the spring of 1986, and planning to co-sponsor another in Singapore in the spring of 1987. The *Study Guides* and *Standards of Practice Handbook* have been translated into Japanese and a project is underway in Japan to translate *Managing Investment Portfolios*. These are initial and important steps toward meeting the challenge articulated by John Templeton.

In addition, the Institute is working closely with the Societies in the United Kingdom and Japan and is affiliated with established Societies in Europe and the Pacific Rim, through the European Federation, the Asian Society and the International Coordinating Committee. Professionalization transcends national boundaries and language differences. It is a world-wide goal and the Institute is looked upon internationally as the example to affiliate with or to follow.

But much remains for the Institute to accomplish in North America. Recognition of the Institute and the CFA is well established in the Canadian financial and regulatory community. Through the efforts of the staff, trustees and members, the Institute and CFA designation are receiving increasing recognition in the larger and more diverse U.S. financial and regulatory community. The Institute is a major influence in the academic community through the CFA sponsored publications and through its cooperation with the Financial Management Association. The CFA study and examination experience is considered by many as the investment training program for investment analysts and investment managers.

Two very important events have taken place in 1986 that are a testimony to the current "stride" of the Institute and the opportunity for the coordination of research and professional efforts within the North American investment community.

Charles A. D'Ambrosio, CFA, editor of the *Financial Analysts Journal* and the *CFA Digest,* wrote an eloquent editorial in the January/February 1986 issue of the *Journal.* He called on the investment profession to renew its commitment to both pure and applied research. At the same time the trustees of the Financial Analysts Research Foundation were completing an evaluation of their own research efforts. At their June 1986 meeting, the Foundation Board under the leadership of James R. Vertin, CFA, requested that the research objectives of the Foundation be absorbed by and integrated with the Institute better to serve the needs of the profession. The prospects for this renewed and reformatted research effort offer real promise for the future.

In May 1986, I wrote a letter to all members of the Institute regarding a new chapter and what I hope will be a new beginning in the relationship between the Institute and the Financial Analysts Federation. With Pete Morley, our tireless president and CEO, serving in that joint capacity for both organizations, the Institute and Federation have a unique opportunity to serve the profession as "partners in professionalism." This partnership respects the autonomy sought by the founding fathers to insulate the Institute from organizational politics and insure "national" membership. But it recognizes the overlapping membership of the two organizations and the need for efficient and effective coordination of the efforts of each organization. The mission statement of the two organizations are being clarified to reflect the Federation's responsibilities for representation of its members and the profession in regulatory, legislative and professional affairs as well as the Institute's responsibilities for education and accreditation of candidates and members.

This relationship is not without its risks. But after careful consideration of both the risks and rewards, the boards of both organizations and the Federation delegates unanimously approved the joint leadership position. As James N. von Germeten, CFA, vice chairman of the Institute and Frederick L.

Muller, CFA, vice chairman of the Federation, both told their respective boards, this is the right time and Pete Morley is the right person. The profession and members will reap the benefits.

Pete, in his new joint leadership role, has initiated the foundation of a joint subsidiary, Financial Analysts Programs, to provide administrative and program support services for both organizations. The efficiencies realized should free up resources for professional programs and support the coordination between the two organizations.

As analysts and investment managers, we are constantly surveying the future. This history has documented where the Institute is today, how it got here and who played key roles in its development. A discussion of where the Institute is going in the future can be drawn from the strategic plan, which in turn is directed by the member surveys. This feedback and planning process in turn directs and establishes priorities for trustee and staff effort.

The key elements in the Institute's current strategic plan are:

1. Promote the Institute's mission, which is the development, certification, maintenance and dissemination of the body of knowledge prescribed for higher educational standards in the fields of investment analysis and investment management.
2. Sponsor, maintain, and enforce, along with the Financial Analysts Federation, the Code of Ethics and Standards of Professional Conduct.
3. Develop the total scope of professional services to CFAs, with particular emphasis on continuing education/ accreditation.
4. Develop and implement a comprehensive marketing and public relations program to promote the recognition and distinction of the CFA Charter and of the CFA Candidate and Accreditation Programs.
   a. Increase the awareness and self-esteem of existing members toward the quality and value of their charter and the total scope of services provided to them by the ICFA.

b. Build a much greater recognition, familiarity, and "name" identification of the CFA Charter and what it stands for among employers, other investors, educators, regulators, and the public at large.

c. Develop a greater internal and external understanding of the two equal priorities of service that flow from the body of knowledge: Candidate Curriculum, Examination, and Certification; and Continuing Education/Accreditation.

5. Determine and implement modifications and changes in the current organizational structure of the ICFA, if they are needed, in the light of the key issues affecting the Institute's future activities. Such key issues include:

a. estimated five year membership growth

b. expanding continuing education and accreditation programs

c. longer-term strategy, for greater international exposure

d. effective delivery of services to members

e. coordination and cooperation with the Financial Analysts Federation and other professional investment-related organizations

f. sponsorship of pure and applied research to expand and document further the body of knowledge.

6. Ongoing evaluation of the quality, effectiveness, and consistency of the Candidate Curriculum and Examination Programs in light of:

a. the changing dynamics of the investment management industry

b. the interest in internationalization of markets and professional standards

c. the trend toward specialization by existing and prospective CFA candidates.

7. Develop and implement a long-term international strategy for the ICFA, designed to achieve a truly international scope for the Institute, its services, and its membership.

This plan is the blueprint for the staff, trustees and members as the Institute "strides" toward its future anniversaries. The past is but a prologue.

The success of the Institute to date reflects the efforts and accomplishments of:

People who have been concerned about their profession;
People who have cared about the profession; and
People who have wanted to contribute their time and talent to better themselves and their profession.

The future of the Institute is in the hands of the current generation of such people. Opportunities to build on the legacy of the past are enormous, and the resolve to do so is well established. The organization, planning and staffing are largely in place. With increased concern for protection of the rights and interests of the investing public, self-regulation and professional competency are needed as much or more so today than they were in early 1960s when the Institute was founded. The potential for service to the profession and the investing public is the guiding beacon for the Institute of Chartered Financial Analysts.

John L. Maginn, CFA
Omaha, Nebraska
July, 1986

APPENDIXES

APPENDIX A

GUIDELINES TO THE CODE OF ETHICS

1. The Chartered Financial Analyst shall maintain high standards of conduct in all aspects of his relationships with the public, customers, clients, employers, employees and associates and corporate management and other sources of information, that he will give meticulous consideration to both the letter and spirit of the law and cooperate fully with regulation by government agencies, stock exchanges and industry groups.

2. The Chartered Financial Analyst shall conduct himself in such manner that transactions for clients have priority over personal transactions and such personal transactions shall not in any way operate adversely to the interests of clients. Full disclosure should be made of any individual or firm interest in the specific securities recommended for purchase or sale.

3. The Chartered Financial Analyst shall not undertake independent practice in competition with his employer.

4. The Chartered Financial Analyst shall not pay fees or commissions to others for recommending his service unless such payment is fully disclosed to the public or the client.

5. The Chartered Financial Analyst shall exercise care in borrowing from material prepared by other analysts, giving full credit where due, and being extremely careful to avoid plagiarism.

6. While the Chartered Financial Analyst is encouraged to display his diploma and to use the C.F.A. designation in a dignified and appropriate manner in keeping with the customary procedure of other similar professional designations, he shall not use it to draw attention to his personal professional attainments or services through the media of paid newspaper or journal advertisements.

7. Violations of the Code of Ethics or "Guidelines" will be regarded as cause for termination by appropriate action of the Board of Trustees of the Institute of Chartered Financial Analyst's right to use the C.F.A. designation.

APPENDIX B

BASIC PLANNING DOCUMENT

Report of Research and Publications Committee on Requirements for Examinations of Candidates

During the past year, The Research and Publications Committee has been divided into several groups to review the examination requirements for each of the C.F.A. examinations and the material available to the Council of Examiners on which to base examination questions. The purpose of this report is to summarize the results of this study and to make recommendations for further action.

Two general conclusions have emerged from the deliberations of this Committee:

1. The purpose of the examinations as part of the procedure leading to the award of a charter is to assure that the holder of a charter has a comprehensive grasp of a body of knowledge that covers the field of financial analysis. Other requirements review the candidate's experience and moral character. No examination procedure can test whether this body of knowledge will be applied or whether the charter holder will possess the talent and ability to be a successful analyst.

2. The present overall plan leading to the award of a charter should be maintained, i.e., over at least three annual periods based on study guides, or books of readings and supplementary written material.

The remainder of this report will be divided into five sections, covering each of the following areas: ethical standards, economics, accounting, financial analysis, and portfolio management. Each section reviews the knowledge the candidate is assumed to have prior to starting his preparation for Examination I. If these requirements are not met, supplementary study will be necessary. The remaining parts of each section will consider the recommended areas to be covered in each examination. No consideration has been given to the area of organization and operation of a research department, as this is an administrative function and it is recommended that it be dropped from the examination content.

I—ETHICAL STANDARDS

Pre-Examination Requirements: It is assumed that all candidates before they begin the examination procedure are of sound moral quality and that their character and reputation have been checked as a part of the registration procedure.

Examination I: Ethical conduct cannot be tested any more than can the chances of analytical success. However, at each stage of the examination procedure, the candidate can be confronted with specific day-to-day ethical problems to insure that he can recognize the problems and know how to deal with them. In Examination I, the problems would cover ethical considerations in dealing with the public, employers, associates, and fellow analysts, which would be the contacts that a junior analyst ordinarily would be expected to have.

Examination II: At this level of experience the analyst has more customer and corporate management contact. Therefore it is recommended that the questions cover ethical considerations in dealing with customers, clients, corporate management, and other sources of information.

Examination III: At this level of experience, the analyst is presumably in a position to supervise the work of others. Therefore it recommended that he be examined on the ethical problems that arise in the administration of standards and the disciplinary action required. He should also be familiar with securities laws and regulations, so that he should know when to seek advice of counsel when a marginal legal issue is involved.

II—ECONOMICS

Pre-Examination Requirements: Because more and more of the candidates have done their university work in the postwar period, it can be assumed that the candidate is familiar with macroeconomic analysis. He is also assumed to have had courses in economic theory and history, and money and banking (including the operation of the Federal Reserve System).

Examination I: The objective at this stage is to insure that the candidate is *familiar with* the economic information available that is useful in the analysis of economic developments and securities. These tools would include:

1. National income accounts.
2. Flow of funds data.
3. Input-output analysis.
4. National Bureau indicators as reported in *Business Cycle Developments.*
5. Budget of the U.S.—New concepts.
6. Aggregate corporate profits measures.
7. Long-term trends in stock and bond prices.
8. Aggregate price movements, i.e., consumer and wholesale price indexes.

Examination II: At this stage, the analyst should be able to demonstrate his ability to *use* these economic tools for the analysis of industries and individual securities. Consequently he should be able to demonstrate familiarity with the following areas:

1. Cyclical and long-term growth trends in the economy.
2. Money market analysis.
3. Fiscal policy.
4. Supply and demand for funds.
5. More detail on aggregate profits data.
   a. Different measures of profits, e.g., tax reported, shareholder reported, national income account basis.

b. Unit cost data in manufacturing and in corporate non-financial area.

Examination III: At this stage, the analyst should be able to use economic analysis in determining investment policy. He also should be able to relate economic analysis to its impact on the securities markets (stocks and bonds) and the earnings trends of companies and industries. The emphasis here will be more on contemporary economic issues and their investment implications.

III — ACCOUNTING

Pre-Examination Requirements: It is assumed that before an analyst is hired, he has had at least the equivalent of two years of accounting at the college level.

Examination I: The first examination should be aimed at determining whether the candidate can use his knowledge of accounting for financial analysis because the analyst has at his disposal not the internal accounting records of the firm but only published information. He especially should become familiar with the following areas:

1. Inventory valuation and its impact on earnings.
2. Depreciation accounting and its impact on earnings.
3. Adjustment of earnings for splits, stock dividends, and the treatment of rights, warrants, and conversion features.
4. Deferred tax accounting.
5. Treatment of intangibles.
6. Ratio analysis.
7. Sources and uses of funds.
8. Analysis of the balance sheet.

Examination II: The analyst at this level should indicate more familiarity with recent Accounting Principles Board opinions in controversial areas. He should also be aware of accounting problems for conglomerates and for acquisitions.

Examination III: This area should be an extension of Examination II, with emphasis on current controversies in accounting treatment.

IV—FINANCIAL ANALYSIS

Pre-Examination Requirements: The candidate is assumed to have some background in this area equivalent to a master's degree in economics or business administration. He should therefore be familiar with the following areas:

1. History of economic and social change.
2. Corporate finance.
3. Development of corporate financial policy.
4. History of economic institutions.
5. History of the business corporations.
6. Public policy toward regulation and antitrust.
7. Separation of ownership and control of corporations, and the results.
8. Corporate concentration.
9. Growth of the institutional investor.
10. Elementary mathematics and statistics.

Examination I: The analyst at this stage does not exercise a great degree of judgement, but he should be able to prepare factual information to be used as a basis for decisions. His abilities should be tested in the following areas:

1. Sources of investment information.
2. Presentation of a stock analysis.
3. Presentation of a bond analysis.
4. Factual evaluation of management, e.g., corporate record, reports, competitive position, control of company.
5. Instruments of investing.
6. Further development of mathematics and statistical background, including use of the computer and the available computer data for security analysis.

Examination II: The major thrust of Examination II is in this area, because the analyst should now be able to prepare reports that separate facts, estimates, opinions, and conclusions. He should be able to deal effectively with the following areas:

1. Estimated returns of various securities under varying conditions.
2. Industry appraisal and evaluation.
3. Projections of earnings and dividends—single point and probability distributions.
4. Discounted cash flow and other valuation techniques, including relative value analysis.
5. Valuation of growth stocks and impact of nonfinancial developments, e.g., research and scientific developments.
6. Assessment of value of dividends, retained earnings, and book value.
7. Qualitative and quantitative measures of risk.
8. Analysis of stock prices and identification of areas of speculation.
9. Capital budgeting and cost of capital.
10. Evaluation of management—personal appraisal.
11. Further development of mathematics and statistics and use of computer in analysis.

Examination III: Financial analysis at this level deals primarily with selection of securities and falls more in the province of portfolio management.

V—PORTFOLIO MANAGEMENT

Pre-Examination Requirements: No prior knowledge of portfolio management is assumed necessary.

Examination I: It is recommended that some familiarity with portfolio management be required in Examination I, because the beginning analyst should understand the problems of the user of his reports. He should therefore have a general familiarity with the following areas:

1. Objectives for investing.
2. Appropriateness of various investment instruments to meet objectives.
3. Problems of marketability.
4. Problems of supervision.
5. Characteristics of securities:
   a. Earnings and dividend patterns.
   b. Comparability with patterns in market place.
   c. Comparability with other securities.
   d. Return.
   e. Quality.
   f. Predictability.

Examination II: At this level, the candidate should have a familiarity with the following principles of portfolio construction:

1. Risk.
2. Diversification concepts.
3. Return.
4. Variability and quality of rate of return.

Examination III: The main thrust of this examination is in portfolio management. The candidate therefore should be familiar with the following areas:

1. Portfolio problems of institutions and individuals, including those now covered (investment companies, banks, insurance companies, and fiduciaries) and expanded to include foundations, endowment funds, hedge funds, and profit sharing funds.
2. Technical and market analysis.
3. Formula plans.
4. Mathematical approaches to portfolio management.
5. Performance measurement.
6. Block trading and other trading problems.

7. Management of bond portfolios of various types.
8. Tax planning.

RECOMMENDATIONS

Assuming Approval of the Trustees of the outline above, the following recommendations for future action are made:

1. The present readings in the C.F.A. Readings book and the Study Guides be reviewed and listed under the appropriate headings above.
2. This analysis be resubmitted to the Research and Publications Committee to determine which readings are appropriate, whether they are the best available, which should be dropped, where additions are needed, and where gaps in the available literature exist.
3. Where gaps exist, the C.F.A. Research Foundation and the *Financial Analysts Journal* seek to have appropriate articles written.
4. The resulting recommendations be submitted to the Executive Director for revision in the C.F.A. Study Guides in both content and recommended readings.

Respectfully submitted,

Edmund A. Mennis, C.F.A.
Chairman
Research and
 Publications Committee

APPENDIX C

THE INSTITUTE OF CHARTERED FINANCIAL ANALYSTS

BOARD OF TRUSTEES

PAST PRESIDENTS AND CHAIRMEN

APPENDIX D

THE C. STEWART SHEPPARD AWARD

1976   C. Stewart Sheppard
A. Moyer Kulp, CFA
George M. Hansen, CFA
M. Dutton Morehouse, CFA
David G. Watterson, CFA

1977   Gilbert H. Palmer, CFA

1978   Edmund A. Mennis, CFA

1979   Frank E. Block, CFA

1980   Robert D. Milne, CFA

1981   Mary Petrie, CFA

1982   Marshall D. Ketchum, CFA
Bion B. Howard, CFA

1983   William A. Cornish, CFA

1984   Alfred C. Morley, CFA
James R. Vertin, CFA

1985   Richard W. Lambourne, CFA

1986   Charles D. Ellis, CFA

EXHIBITS I & II

EXHIBIT I

Required Exam Topics, 1968 CFA Brochure

Examination I — Investment Principles

Financial Accounting
Basic Quantitative Analysis
Basic Economic Analysis
Principles of Financial Analysis
Financial Instruments and Institutions
Ethics

Examination II — Applied Security Analysis

Practical Applications of Financial Analysis
Economic Growth and Business Fluctuations
Ethics

Examination III — Investment Management Decision-Making

Portfolio Management
Organization and Administration of Investment Activities
Common Stock Policy
Fixed Income Securities Analysis
Security Selections
Economic Issues
Ethics

EXHIBIT II
General Topic Outline, 1969

Candidate Level I   II   III

ACCOUNTING

Principles and Construction of Accounting Statements:
- Balance sheet
- Income statement
- Sources and uses
- Other

Analysis of Accounting Statements:
- Income statement and balance sheet analysis
- Comparative company analysis
- Inventory evaluation
- Depreciation accounting
- Deferred tax accounting
- Treatment of intangibles
- Stock splits and dividends
- Rights, warrants, convertibles
- Ratio and coverage analysis
- Other

Current Accounting Principles and Practices:
- AICPA opinions
- Controversial areas
- Acquisitions and mergers
- Conglomerates

ECONOMICS

Basic Principles and Source Materials:
- GNP and national income accounts
- The monetary system
- The fiscal system
- The price system
- Flow-of-funds
- Input-output analysis
- Aggregate profit measures
- Indicator series analysis
- Long-term trends in stock and bond prices

Economic Analysis and Forecasting:
- Input-output applications
- Corporate profits forecasting
- Indicator series applications
- Supply and demand of funds in the market
- Economic fluctuations and long-term trends

Economic Policy:
- Monetary policy
- Fiscal policy
- Balance of payments and international policy
- Money supply
- Antitrust legislation
- Employment policy
- Growth of the institutional investor

FINANCIAL ANALYSIS

Principles of Financial Analysis:
- Sources of information
- Financial instruments

Candidate Level I   II   III

- Financial institutions
- Common stock analysis
- Fixed income security analysis
- Management appraisal
- Quantitative techniques

Applied Financial Analysis:
- Industry appraisal and evaluation
- Dividends and earnings evaluation and projection
- Valuation techniques
- Risk analysis—qualitative and quantitative
- Market and price analysis and areas of speculation
- Capital budgeting

PORTFOLIO MANAGEMENT

Objectives:
- Individuals
- Institutions
  - investment companies
  - foundations and endowment funds
  - pension funds and profit-sharing plans
  - trust funds
  - fire and casualty insurance companies
  - life insurance companies
  - commercial banks
  - hedge funds

Construction:
- Security selection
- Diversification
- Marketability
- Risk
- Return

Timing and Formula Plans
Bond Portfolio Problems
Performance Measurement
Trading Problems
Tax Planning
Supervision
Quantitative Techniques for Portfolio Management
Computer Applications
Regulation

ETHICAL STANDARDS

C.F.A Responsibilities:
- Public
- Customers and clients
- Employers
- Associates
- Other analysts
- Corporate management
- Other sources of information

Professionalization
Administering Ethical Policy
Security Laws and Regulations